P9-CDN-960

SOME ASPECTS OF THE GREEK GENIUS

MACMILLAN AND CO., Limited
LONDON · BOMBAY · CALCUTTA
MADRAS · MELBOURNE

THE MACMILLAN COMPANY
NEW YORK · BOSTON · CHICAGO
DALLAS · SAN FRANCISCO

THE MACMILLAN CO. OF CANADA, Ltd.
TORONTO

SOME ASPECTS

OF

THE GREEK GENIUS

BY

S. H. BUTCHER

HON. D.LITT. OXFORD, HON. LITT.D. DUBLIN
HON. LL.D. GLASGOW AND EDINBURGH
LATE PROFESSOR OF GREEK IN THE UNIVERSITY OF EDINBURGH
FORMERLY FELLOW OF TRINITY COLLEGE, CAMBRIDGE
AND OF UNIVERSITY COLLEGE, OXFORD

MACMILLAN AND CO., LIMITED
ST. MARTIN'S STREET, LONDON
1929

First Edition 1891.
Second Edition 1893.
Third Edition 1904.
Fourth Edition 1916.
Reprinted 1929.

PRINTED IN GREAT BRITAIN

PREFACE TO THE THIRD EDITION

NO material changes will be found in this volume, though some slight additions and corrections have been made. The essay on "The Dawn of Romanticism in Greek Poetry" was introduced into the second edition. The same subject has recently received interesting and independent treatment from my friend Professor W. R. Hardie, in a chapter entitled "The Vein of Romance in Greek and Roman Literature," which forms one of his *Lectures on Classical Subjects* (Macmillan and Co., 1903). It seems worth while to remind classical readers that, though we cannot efface the broad differences which are compendiously expressed in the terms "classical" and "romantic" poetry, the lines of distinction are not so hard and sharp as we are sometimes inclined to imagine.

Stray touches of modern sentiment, and even of what may be called "romanticism," are met with already in the strictly classical period of Greek literature; and these anticipations of a new era occur with increasing frequency in the later Greek poets. Of the literary products of the Hellenistic age few complete specimens survive. Yet the comparatively scanty materials we possess, combined with what we know from other sources, enable us to draw certain general conclusions. Nature and Love—these are the two new motives which now enter into imaginative literature: or, if the motives themselves are not wholly new, the mode of poetic utterance is perceptibly altered. There is an inwardness of tone, a reflectiveness, a heightened sensibility—often indicating a vague disquiet of the mind and betraying itself in accents of longing or regret—that may be traced also in other regions of feeling. Some detailed illustrations of this mood are given in the essay itself.

September 1904.

CONTENTS

WHAT WE OWE TO GREECE

THE question to which I would here attempt an answer in rudest outline is, What do we owe to Greece? what is the secret of her power and permanence? what of her own has she contributed to the world's common store? what is her place in history? If we find, as I think we shall, that Hellenism has not given us enough to live by, yet we shall also see how greatly they misread the mind of Greece who think to become Hellenic by means of eccentricity tinged with vice.

First, then, the Greeks, before any other people of antiquity, possessed the love of knowledge for its own sake. To see things as they really are, to discern their meanings and adjust their relations, was with them an instinct and a passion. Their methods in science and philosophy might be very faulty, and their conclusions often absurd, but they had that fearlessness of intellect which is the first condition of seeing truly. Poets and philosophers alike looked with unflinching eye on all that met them, on man and the world, on life and death. They interrogated Nature, and sought to wrest her secret from her, without misgiving and without afterthought. Greece, first smitten with the passion for truth, had the courage to put faith in reason, and in following its guidance to take no count of consequences. "Those," says Aristotle, "who would rightly judge the truth, must be arbitrators and not litigants."[1] "Let us follow the argument whithersoever it leads,"[2] may be taken not only as the motto of the Platonic philosophy, but as expressing one side of the Greek genius.

The Eastern nations, speaking generally, had loved to move in a region of twilight, content with that half-knowledge which stimulates the religious sense. They had thought it impious to draw aside the veil which hides God from man. They had shrunk in holy awe from the study of causes, from inquiries into origin, from explaining the perplexed ways of the universe. Ignorance had been the sacred duty of the layman. Scientific

[1] Arist. *de Caelo* i. 10. 279 b 11, δεῖ διαιτητὰς ἀλλ' οὐκ ἀντιδίκους εἶναι τοὺς μέλλοντας τἀληθὲς κρίνειν ἱκανῶς.

[2] Plat. *Laws* ii. 667 A, ὁ λόγος ὅπῃ φέρει, ταύτῃ πορευώμεθα. *Rep.* iii. 394 D, ὅπῃ ἂν ὁ λόγος ὥσπερ πνεῦμα φέρῃ, ταύτῃ ἰτέον.

questioning and discovery could hardly exist where, as in many parts of the East, each fresh gain of earth was thought to be so much robbery of heaven.

At the moment when Greece first comes into the main current of the world's history, we find a quickened and stirring sense of personality, and a free play of intellect and imagination. The oppressive silence with which Nature and her unexplained forces had brooded over man is broken. Not that the Greek temper is irreverent, or strips the universe of mystery. The mystery is still there and felt, and has left many undertones of sadness in the bright and heroic records of Greece; but the sense of mystery has not yet become mysticism. One writer, it is true, whose temper was that of the mystic, appeared in Greece in the first half of the fifth century B.C., Empedocles of Agrigentum. At once poet, priest, and philosopher, skilled in medicine and a student of natural science, this striking and poetic figure passed in pomp through the towns of Sicily, a healer of the diseases both of mind and body. He speaks of himself as a heavenly spirit, exiled from the company of the blest, who for the taint of crime is condemned to be incarnate upon earth

As a fallen intellect he has lost the full and unbroken vision of the universe; still he is gifted with an insight beyond common men into the truth of things, and speaks with lofty pity of mankind, who, knowing nothing, "boast that they have found out the whole—an idle boast; for this the eye of man hath not seen, nor hath his ear heard, nor can his mind conceive it."[1] He himself shrinks from learning more than it is given to human wisdom to know. He would tell only such things "as creatures of a day may reverently hear," and prays the Muse who inspires him to "guide her light car from the house of Holiness."[2] Such cautious reverence, alternating with bold utterances in moments of illumination, is rarely met with in Greek literature. Greek thinkers are not afraid that they may be guilty of prying into the hidden things of the gods. They hold frank companionship with thoughts that had paralysed Eastern nations into dumbness or inactivity, and

[1] Emped. 6-8.

τὸ δ' ὅλον μὰψ εὔχεται εὑρεῖν·
οὕτως οὔτ' ἐπιδερκτὰ τάδ' ἀνδράσιν οὔτ' ἐπακουστὰ
οὔτε νόῳ περιληπτά.

[2] *Ib.* 13-14.

ἄντομαι ὧν θέμις ἐστὶν ἐφημερίοισιν ἀκούειν,
πέμπε παρ' Εὐσεβίης ἐλάουσ' εὐήνιον ἅρμα.

in their clear gaze there is no ignoble terror. Inroads, indeed, there were at times from the East of strange gods and fanatical rites; and half-lit spaces always remained in which forms of faith or ritual, lower as well as higher than the popular creed, took shelter; but, on the whole, we are henceforth in an upper and serener air in which man's spiritual and intellectual freedom is assured.

"Know thyself" is the answer which the Greek offers to the Sphinx's riddle. How truly does all Greek literature and art respond to the command! When philosophy had as yet scarcely begun to look inward, the poets—Homer, Pindar, Aeschylus, Sophocles—with large and impartial observation had reflected human life. Euripides, indeed, stands on the confines of a new poetic age. He widened the range of poetic imitation, and made his tragedy to reflect more closely "the whole tragi-comedy of life."[1] The old classic clearness of outline and precision of form are already being blurred. The image is presented to us in shifting lights and through a turbid or refracting medium. There is an intrusion of the pathetic element, a portrayal of transient and unruly emotions, for the better exhibition of which the poet seeks out

[1] Plat. *Phil.* 50 B, τῇ τοῦ βίου ξυμπάσῃ τραγῳδίᾳ καὶ κωμῳδίᾳ.

striking situations. He projects his own personal trouble and the colour of his times into his art. A sense is left of contradiction and disquiet, of vague and inarticulate wants. The doubtful gleams of a romantic light already play over the surface of the Euripidean tragedy; the echoes are heard of a music dying away in the distance and baffling the ears which are strained to catch it. Euripides provokes questioning and reflection; he does not, like Aeschylus and Sophocles, lead to a reverent acquiescence in the mystery of things. But they and he alike look with unaverted eye on the mixed spectacle of life, and accept with fortitude whatever may be appointed. "Now observe," says Mr. Ruskin—his primary reference being to Homer—"that in their dealings with all these subjects the Greeks never shrink from horror; down to its uttermost depths, to its most appalling physical detail, they strive to sound the secrets of sorrow. For them there is no passing by on the other side, no turning away the eyes to vanity from pain. . . . Whether there be consolation for them or not, neither apathy nor blindness shall be their saviour: if for them, thus knowing the facts of the grief of earth, any hope, relief, or triumph may hereafter seem possible,—

well; but if not, still hopeless, reliefless, eternal, the sorrow shall be met face to face."[1]

But to the Greeks "Know thyself" meant not only to know *man*, but—a less pleasing task—to know *foreigners*. And to this study they were impelled not solely, or even chiefly, by a commercial and gain-seeking instinct, such as moved the Phoenicians, but by a single-hearted desire to know. It was a new thing in the world. The people of ancient India did not care to penetrate beyond their mountain barriers and to know their neighbours. The Egyptians, though in certain branches of science they had made progress—in medicine, in geometry, in astronomy—had acquired no scientific geography, for they kept to themselves. But the Greeks were travellers. Of Odysseus it is said: "Many were the men whose towns he saw and whose mind he learned";[2] and in this respect he is typical of his race. We are often told that the Greeks were exclusive; and their phrase "barbarian" for a foreigner looks a little ugly and contemptuous. But the invidious meaning was acquired only by degrees, and not, perhaps, without reason; in any case it is a less

[1] *Modern Painters*, v. 215.

[2] *Odyss.* i. 3.

invidious term than that of "devils," by which many Easterns have designated their neighbours. And what is more significant, Aristotle thought it worth his while to analyse and describe the constitutions of a hundred and fifty-eight states, including in his survey not only Greek states but those of the barbarian world. He was the first student of what we call Comparative Politics.

The ripe science of Aristotle may be found already in germ in the history of Herodotus. While his history is marching forward on epic lines and with quickening speed to the great conflict between the West and the East, between the Greeks and the Barbarians, yet he has no hard words for the Barbarians. He can view them with candid surprise and impartiality. There is no pause but no haste. He finds time to linger by the way, and exhibits the open-eyed delight of a child who is introduced for the first time into a strange world, where everything, great and small, is alike interesting and worthy of an intent regard. With him we trace the courses of rivers, the movements of tribes; we touch and handle rare objects of nature or of art; we wander through temples hitherto unexplored, we hear him questioning the priests in a tone whose secular curiosity is tempered only by a native piety. There is more here than the unembarrassed wonder of childhood; there is doubt as well as wonder, reflection as well as observation; he compares his reports, he weighs his evidence, he is conscious of his own office as an inquirer after truth. A fact interests him simply because it is true, apart from its emotional or poetic value. Nor does he merely note the facts, he seeks to discover the law which governs them. This law has generally a religious basis. "The providence of the deity"[1] reveals itself even in the habits of the animal kingdom; and to acts of divine intervention he ascribes the more impressive of human events. Yet in spite of his belief in a jealous God, who humbles human greatness and "suffers none but himself to be haughty," the genius of criticism, the spirit of science, is already awake.

It was the privilege of the Greeks to discover the sovereign efficacy of reason. They entered on the pursuit of knowledge with a sure and joyous instinct. Baffled and puzzled they might be, but they never grew weary of the quest. The speculative faculty which reached its height in Plato and Aristotle, was, when we make due

[1] Herod. iii. 108, *τοῦ θείου ἡ προνοίη*.

allowance for time and circumstance, scarcely less eminent in the Ionian philosophers; and it was Ionia that gave birth to an idea, which was foreign to the East, but has become the starting-point of modern science,—the idea that Nature works by fixed laws. A fragment of Euripides speaks of him as "happy who has learned to search into causes," who "discerns the deathless and ageless order of nature, whence it arose, the how and the why."[1] The early poet-philosophers of Ionia gave the impulse which has carried the human intellect forward across the line which separates empirical from scientific knowledge; and the Greek precocity of mind in this direction, unlike that of the Orientals, had in it the promise of uninterrupted advance in the future—of great discoveries in mathematics, geometry, experimental physics, in medicine also and physiology. Already in Heraclitus (*circ.* 513 B.C.) the one thing per-

[1] Eurip. Fr. (Nauck 902)—

> *ὄλβιος ὅστις τῆς ἱστορίας*
> *ἔσχε μάθησιν . . . .*
> *ἀλλ' ἀθανάτου καθορῶν φύσεως*
> *κόσμον ἀγήρω, πῇ τε συνέστη*
> *καὶ ὅπῃ καὶ ὅπως.*

Here *ἱστορία* bears its earliest sense of "research," or "search after truth." Cp. its use in the opening words of the history of Herodotus.

manent in a world of change is the law which governs that change. The physical order of the universe is under the guardianship of the same powers that uphold the moral order. "Helios will not overpass his appointed bounds, or the Erinyes, the ministers of justice, will find him out."[1] The poetic form under which the thought is here expressed is adapted to a prevalent sentiment, which long lingered, that man might indeed overstep the limits of existence and violate nature's order, but not with impunity. The poets contained signal examples of the penalties inflicted on misguided mortals who had raised the dead or otherwise encroached upon the prerogatives of the gods. But by the middle of the fifth century B.C. the general conception of law in the physical world was firmly established in the mind of Greek thinkers. Even the more obscure phenomena of disease were brought within the rule. Hippocrates, writing about a malady which was common among the Scythians and was thought to be preternatural, says: "As for me I think that these maladies are divine like all others, but that

[1] Plutarch, *de Exilio* 11, "Ηλιος γὰρ οὐχ ὑπερβήσεται μέτρα, φησὶν ὁ Ἡράκλειτος· εἰ δὲ μή, Ἐρινύες μιν δίκης ἐπίκουροι ἐξευρήσουσιν.

none is more divine or more human than another. Each has its natural principle, and none exists without its natural cause."[1]

Again, the Greeks set themselves to discover a rational basis for conduct. Rigorously they brought their actions to the test of reason, and that not only by the mouth of philosophers, but through their poets, historians, and orators. Thinking and doing, "the spirit of counsel and might,"—clear thought and noble action—did not to the Greek mind stand opposed. The antithesis rather marks a period when the Hellenic spirit was past its prime, and had taken a one-sided bent. The Athenians of the Periclean age, in whom we must recognise the purest embodiment of Hellenism, had in truth the peculiar power which Thucydides claims for them, of thinking before they acted and of acting also. In the mouth of Pericles are placed the words: "Debate, we hold, does not mar action; the mischief is rather setting to work without being first enlightened."[2] And among the ideas common to Thucydides and Demosthenes this is one—that reason is a formative and conquering power; that

[1] Hippocr. *περὶ ἀέρων, ὑδάτων, τόπων*, ch. 22.

[2] Thucyd. ii. 40.

a strong and clear intelligence can prevail over outward circumstances, and can shape events ; that victory is assured to those who see things as they are and shun illusion, and who at the same time summon to the aid of thought a sustained and courageous energy. In the divorce between thought and deed, between speech and action, Demosthenes truly saw the flaw that was destined fatally to impair Greek conduct and character. In the best times Greek thought did not spend itself in barren effort. Wisdom and heroism, elsewhere found apart, were combined by the Greeks, even as Pallas, goddess of war, was goddess also of counsel.

Thought had become fully conscious of itself in Greece some time before it found the appropriate vehicle of expression in prose. It was not till the sixth century B.C. that writing, so long known in the East but scarcely emancipated from religion, was widely used in Greece. Under this new influence prose literature had its first beginnings. Prose, like poetry, was at first a secret in the possession of a few,—an art confined to a close guild of craftsmen. In the joy of discovery men played with the new weapon, tested its unknown powers, and saw no limit to its wonder-working capacities. It was a critical and decisive moment for literature. Of those who professed the new art some devoted themselves to a minute cult of form, treating language not as the willing servant of thought, but as an independent and sovereign power. For an instant it seemed doubtful whether educated taste, following in the steps of Gorgias and his school, would abandon itself to phrase-making and poetic ornament; whether literary prose starting on a wrong course might worship form and pursue beauty at the expense of truth and seek to dazzle by means of false oppositions and subtleties. Over-subtlety was the vice to which the Greek intellect was most inclined. Thought and the expression of thought were always menaced by the love of formal antithesis and of fine-drawn distinctions—"Graecorum ille morbus" as it is called by Seneca: and a deadly disease it proved, for in the sterile controversies of Alexandrian critics and finally in the hair-splitting of Byzantine theologians the stream of Greek literature ran dry. But for the present, and even when the Greeks had ceased to produce their best work, they resisted the dangerous fascination. An unerring perception told them that the beautiful must also be the true, and recalled them back into the way. As in conduct they insisted on an energy which was rational, so in art and in literature they required of beauty that it too should be, before all things, rational.

As a luminous instance of this we may mention their oratory. The Athenians themselves knew the strange magic which gracious speech exercised over them. A people of artists who listened to beautiful language as to music, who hissed a mispronunciation, who loved debate as they did a spectacle—they were aware of their own susceptibilities, and resolved beforehand to be proof against the enchantment. In the presence of a trained speaker their attitude was one of vigilant incredulity. To guard against surprises, to detect sophistries, became an intellectual luxury; and the unimpassioned calm of the normal Attic peroration—the coldness, as moderns might say, the apparent anti-climax—is in some sort a homage that the orator pays to reason: to reason, not to emotion, he addresses the final appeal. To satisfy so exacting an audience no preparatory pains could be too great. The idea now occurred that speech as an instrument of persuasion might be subjected to analysis, that its theory might be unfolded, its practice illustrated, and that men might be taught to be eloquent. It was a new and fruitful idea; for though language as an instrument of thought, language on its scientific and grammatical side, had been subjected to acute analysis in India, yet language as the instrument of persuasion, shaped and moulded into forms that appealed alike to intellect and feeling, and answered the demands both of reason and beauty—from this point of view language had not hitherto been treated. Such a union of the artistic and scientific spirit was the work of Greece.

The language of Greek authors owes its beauty in no slight measure to their directness of vision. They see the object they mean to describe, they do not recall it through the medium of books from literary reminiscence. The sharp outlines of the thought stand visibly before the mind. Even the prose writers have the poetic gift of taking common words and making them seem as if they were newly minted, with edges unworn and their superscription still plain. It was their good fortune to use a language whose first freshness had not yet faded; yet it needed also finished art to preserve unimpaired the primitive energy of words, and to impart a kind of distinction to what was familiar. We speak of the happy ease and grace with which the Greeks wrote, but they themselves thought of their own aptitude more as the result of trained skill than of instinct. It is remarkable how the word *σοφία*, "wisdom," "skill," is selected by them to denote the poetic gift in contexts where we should be disposed to speak of inspiration. Pindar, who more than any other poet insists on the need of inborn faculty, also exalts to the utmost the influence of art. His poetry is a subtle science, which obeys laws of its own, fixed rules, transmitted by the masters of the craft, by which the structure of the rhythm and the handling of the theme are regulated. His flights of imagination are obedient to this skilled guidance. So too in each kind of literary composition invented by the Greeks there are certain controlling traditions, which even genius cannot escape; or rather, which it would not escape even if it could, for it is within the domain of law—*cui servire regnare est*—that genius exercises its sway. The way to originality was felt to lie through a certain self-suppression, which moderns might think was a hampering of free activity. The prose writers as well as the poets subject themselves to the rules of a conscious art, and the perfection of that art is shown in an absence of exaggeration, a delicate spirit of choice, an unobtrusive propriety of diction. The tone is not forced. The effects are produced with the utmost economy of material and are exactly adequate to the occasion. It is as if they acted on the maxim, *Le secret d'ennuyer est de tout dire.* Owing to the very wealth of right words simplicity becomes possible, and the artist is not betrayed. Repose and power are equally combined, and the distinctive quality of the whole composition is revealed rather in the total impression than in isolated felicities of phrase.

In the domain of eloquence the union of the artistic spirit with technical skill was an idea slowly realised. It so happens that Greek oratory, unlike Roman, can be followed step by step through a continuous development. Cicero stands out the one clear figure among the shadowy forms of Roman orators — a roll of names once famous, now known either through the barest fragments or through the distant haze of literary criticism. Demosthenes, isolated as he is in his moral grandeur, is yet, as concerns his style, the orderly birth of his age and of his country. He can be understood only in relation to his predecessors; his place in a series is well defined. But of that series he is also the sum and the completion. The matured civic eloquence was late in appearing and was comprised within a brief period, between the years 354 and 324 B.C. Coincident with the last struggle for independence and thence drawing its inspiration, it seemed to spring in a moment into life and as suddenly to become extinct. But it had, in fact, passed through the preparatory discipline both of the schools and of the law-courts. There it had learnt its pliancy of idiom, its majestic and harmonious phrase, its skilled arrangement of the thoughts, its militant energy. Its forces all stood ready to respond to a great enthusiasm. A double tendency had declared itself in Attic oratory from the outset. Side by side had grown up the scientific and the artistic type. But hitherto there had been no complete fusion. In Demosthenes the two types are combined. The most business-like of orators, he is also the most artistic. Admitting nothing that is not strictly pertinent, disdaining ornament for its own sake, he counts no detail of workmanship unimportant. Practical reason is the groundwork of his speeches, but it is reason alive with passion. The thought, while irresistible in logic, is charged with emotion. Never has there been such a union of force and living fire with literary finish and rhythmical perfection. He passes beyond the particular occasion and the purpose of the moment, and rising above the wrangling of rival politicians extracts from contemporaneous events political truths which human nature ratifies in every age. Few indeed are the orators of modern times whose speeches live as literature; like singers their day is brief, and when their voice is no longer heard they are forgotten. Demosthenes survives and is still a storehouse of political wisdom and a model of civic eloquence. The reason is that to the gifts of the statesman and the orator he added that instinct of the Hellenic mind which craves durable expression even for its passing utterances, and stamps all its creations with the seal of art. What he had to say he so said as to make it of universal acceptation.

Again, in history, the Greeks were the first who combined science and art, reason and imagination. India, till it came in contact with Greece, had next to no chronology. Fable and legend occupied the field, and in place of history there were epics and dramas. China, on the other hand, knew facts and dates enough, and drew up its records with painstaking exactness. The letter and the written word became with them a cult in which government and religion were merged, so that an emperor who meditated a political revolution saw no expedient so good as to burn the books. Chinese history reflects in a manner Chinese civilisation. Their civilisation, we are told, is founded upon reason; but if so, it is a servile and prosaic reason,—it is reason divorced from beauty and from freedom. Their history is not far different; it is careful, encyclopaedic, and unreadable.

Greece discovered another kind of history, in which reason and beauty were reconciled—one which the Romans borrowed, and which has served as a pattern to modern times. Thucydides, as one who has observed the shaping of events and seized their meaning, sets himself to disengage the causes which produce them, and traces them back to their hidden source in character. The shadow of semi-fatalism which rested over the history of Herodotus is removed. History is no longer the result of the vengeance or jealousy of superhuman powers; it becomes the expression of human intelligence, one of the modes in which reason works out its free activity. It is by this method that Thucydides is "philosophic," and almost in the sense in which Aristotle declares poetry to be "more philosophic than history." Thucydides is philosophic, not as a speculative philosopher who has a system to expound, but as one who looks beyond the particular phenomena with which he is dealing, and discerns the universal type in and through the individual.

His history has also poetic affinities. The speakers tell their own tale; the historian maintains an impartial reserve; the events arrange themselves in dramatic sequence and lead up to a tragic catastrophe. Unimaginative history may contain much useful material, but it is not history regarded as literature. Doubtless the inroad of poetry was in ancient times a standing danger to history, and later Greek history was invaded, and with ruinous results, by poetical and rhetorical fiction. Yet history, however much it may approach to science, by a necessity of its nature falls short of science; it is on the borderland between science and poetry. Thucydides with his sceptical intellect and his stern resolve not to quit the ground of solid fact, cannot divest himself of the imaginative genius of his race. His history is dramatic, and in a two-fold way. First through the speeches, which, though they were never delivered as they stand, sum up the thoughts of the representative actors on each occasion. If they do not place before us vivid portraits of the individual speakers, they express the larger lineaments of Spartans or Athenians; they are a mirror of national character revealing itself at significant moments. They are never ornamental accessories, but are in intimate relation with the facts on which they form a lucid commentary, and which through them become generalised truths. The reflections that occur here in the strictly imaginative portion of the work, the view of the situation here unfolded, the analysis of the motives that go to make events —this it is which mainly gives to the history of Thucydides its comprehensive wisdom. Again, he is dramatic in his presentment of facts. Voltaire wished that a history might be written, in which, as in a piece put upon the stage, there should be a dramatic situation,—the unfolding of a story, the tying of a knot, and the *dénouement*. Such a history Thucydides has written. The period of the Peloponnesian war had a well-defined unity of its own. A single great action was here evolved. The facts were full of tragic meaning; all that was required to bring out their inherent grandeur and pathos was that they should be skilfully ordered. "Thucydides," says Professor Jebb,[1] "is dramatic, for instance, when he places the Melian dialogue immediately before the Sicilian expedition. The simple juxtaposition of insolence and ruin is more effective than comment." And further, the Peloponnesian war presents "a definite moment at which the cardinal situation is reversed. . . . That moment is the Sicilian expedition. The supreme test of 'dramatic' quality in a history of the Peloponnesian war must be the power with which the historian has marked the significance of the Sicilian expedition as the tragic 'revolution,' the climax of pity and terror, the decisive reversal. . . . Here, at the point in his story which supplies the crucial test, Thucydides shows that he possesses true dramatic power. By the direct presentment of the facts, not by reflections upon them, he makes us feel all that is tragic in the Sicilian disaster itself, and also all that it means in relation to the larger tragedy of the war."

The application of a clear and fearless intellect to every domain of life was, then, one of the

[1] *Hellenica*, p. 318.

services rendered by Greece to the world. It was connected with the awakening of the lay spirit. In the East the priests had generally held the keys of knowledge. Even writing tended to be a hieratic secret. Literature and science were branches of theology, and their study belonged to the priestly office. Thus, in India the Brahmins had always hidden from the people the sources whence their knowledge was derived. They watched, indeed, the course of discovery and turned it to account, but represented each new discovery as part of a primitive revelation. Still more marked in Egypt was the impress left by the priesthood on all the arts and sciences. In Greece, from the earliest time, the sacerdotal influence is slight. Not that there were no priests, but the priests never became a corporation, still less a caste. Even women might hold the priestly office, an office sometimes conferred by popular election. Theano in the *Iliad* (vi. 300) is appointed by the Trojans to be priestess of Athene. Vows of celibacy were not a necessary condition for the office: personal beauty was sometimes made essential. From the first sight we catch of the priests in Homer, they are attached to certain local worships and do not quit the temple. They do not accompany the army to war. Even in time of peace, the heroes themselves offer the sacrifices which precede the family meal. The priest and the diviner are generally lightly accounted in Homer, and the minstrel or singer is held in higher honour. Nor did the priests penetrate into private life or teach religion. They were not theologians, but sacristans and liturgical functionaries. Not they, but the poets became the educators of youth.

Together with intellectual enfranchisement Greece found also political freedom. In the East, society had fluctuated between despotism and anarchy; if it did not fall under one or other of these forces, it was only, as with the Jews, saved by means of a theocracy. Now, in Greece, though despotisms sprang up, they were never quite of the Eastern type—a single master and a people of slaves; and, moreover, they were quickly followed by reactions. Being, in truth, the negation of all Greek ideas, they were never accepted save after a struggle, and the tyrant knew the insecure tenure of his power. From the outset we see that tyrannies will find no congenial soil in Greece. The king, in Homeric times, is far from being an Asiatic monarch. The chief points of difference are indicated by Aristotle,[1] where he tells us that heroic royalty was established by the free consent of the governed, and the functions attaching to it were determinate: the king was a general and a judge, and presided at sacrificial rites. Willing subjects and limited prerogatives—here we have Western ideas. Heroic royalty has in it the germ of future republics; for the Greek city springs from the independent union of independent wills, it is a self-governing community regulated by law and not by force. One of the recorded sayings of Heraclitus runs thus: "The people should fight for the law as for the city rampart."[2] The Spartan Demaratus thus describes his countrymen to the Great King: "Though free, they are not wholly free. The law for them is a supreme master" (*ἔπεστι γάρ σφι δεσπότης νόμος*).[3] And the Athenian Aeschylus puts into the mouth of the Eumenides the words, "Praise neither the life of anarchy nor the life of despotism."[4] "Unblest freedom from restraint" (to use again the phrase of Aeschylus) was not the Greek conception of a freeman; and those

[1] Aristot. *Pol.* iii. 14. 1285 b 4.

[2] Diog. Laert. ix. 2, *μάχεσθαι χρὴ τὸν δῆμον ὑπὲρ τοῦ νόμου ὅκως ὑπὲρ τείχεος.* [3] Herod. vii. 104. [4] Aesch. *Eum.* 526.

tribes or ἔθνη who had no centres of political life, no settled law and usage, even if of Greek blood, hardly counted as forming part of the Greek brotherhood; they were only a grade above wandering hordes. But still more foreign to Greek sentiment were the great military monarchies which from time to time overshadowed Greek civilisation. To such a monarchy Greece at length succumbed. And the whole force of Demosthenes' genius is spent on marking the contrast between the subjects of such a state and the free citizens of Greece. He is the interpreter of Hellenism as against Barbarism. In the name of free institutions he appeals to the sense of honour and duty, to human dignity, to moral responsibility, to enlightened patriotism—appeals, all of them unmeaning to men who were part of a mere machine, fitted into an iron framework, who knew only of obedience to a master, and for whom the past had no inspiring memories.

The East did not attempt to reconcile the claims of the state and the individual. The pliant genius of Greece first made the effort. In Greece first the idea of the public good, of the free devotion of the citizen to the state, of government in the interests of the governed, of the rights of the individual, took shape. The problem of the relation between the state and the individual was, indeed, very imperfectly solved in Greece. The demands, for instance, of the state were pitched too high and implied a virtue almost heroic in its members. Even in Athens, where individual liberty was most regarded, certain urgent public needs were supplied mainly by the precarious method of private generosity instead of by state organisation. But though the Greeks may not have solved the political problem, they saw that there was a problem to solve, and set about it rationally ; and they were the first to do so. They were gifted with a power, peculiarly Western, of delicate adjustment, of combining principles apparently opposite, of harmonising conflicting claims ; they possessed a sense of measure, a flexibility, a faculty of compromise, opposed to the fatal simplicity with which Eastern politics had been stricken. Not tyranny, not anarchy, satisfied the Greek, but ordered liberty.

Passing now to another side of the Greek genius —their love of Art—let us go back for a few minutes to that early time of which Homer and Herodotus have left us a picture. By land and by sea there came to Hellas the marvels of the East.

Golgos, Idalia, Curium, Larnaka, and Nimroud have yielded to us their treasures, and all tell the same story—the story of the splendour of the East and the wonder of the West. The picture of Herodotus is still fresh; the Phoenician trader—the carrier of the ancient world—voyaging in his black ship, freighting his vessel with the wares of Egypt and Assyria; the landing on the Argive coast; the five days' fare; the throng of eager Hellenes. And those very wares for which they bartered are scattered now throughout the museums of Europe; fantastic carved shells, bronze idols, silver bowls graven with zones of tigers and with hybrid monsters—winged sphinxes, chimaeras, human-headed birds—things born of an unbridled Eastern imagination, and wrought with prolific industry in the valleys of the Nile and the Euphrates. Egyptian art, like Egyptian thought, was, we know, heavy with the incubus of an all-powerful priesthood; it was an elaborate cult of the dead, haunted, half-scared with the shadows of the underworld. It was the art of a people who called their houses "hostelries" (καταλύσεις), places of temporary sojourn, while their tombs they called the "eternal homes."[1] Among their gods

[1] Diodor. Sic. i. 51.

were dog-headed apes, whose animal forms, born of a totemism never wholly extinct, were to later days hybrid symbols, incarnate dogmas; their proportions were conventional, their individuality floating and confused, and their virtue lay rather in size than in symmetry. Assyrian art, on the other hand, was the outcome, and bore the impress, of a despotism not religious but secular. The king was to the Euphrates what the priest was to the Nile. With laborious detail the Assyrian artist inscribes upon the palace walls the story of the monarch's prowess, of his fierce license, of his inhuman courage, of the abject multitude that abase themselves before him. Six thousand square metres are not enough for the tedious iteration. Even the kings are types, not individuals; the artist works by precept, almost by prescription; he is but the lifeless mouthpiece of a system, a servile chronicler, now rising to bombast, now sinking to garrulity.

All this we know in the light of a mature art-criticism; but how is the Greek to fare when some thirty centuries ago he looks on this world of fantastic wonder with child-like eyes? We might tremble for the issue did we not know the sequel. It is as though he said to himself: "I will borrow from this artist of the East his technical skill ; I will learn of him his sleight of hand ; he shall teach me to carve and to grave, to inlay with metal and to fashion with clay." That he did so learn, literature and art alike tell us. The silver bowl which Achilles gave as a prize at the funeral of Patroclus was made by Sidonian artists, and brought by Phoenicians over the sea ; Helen's silver work-basket which ran on wheels was fashioned in Egyptian Thebes. But against the spirit of the East the spirit of the Hellene revolted. To the Egyptian priest he appears to say : "I am a layman ; I worship in the sunshine a god who is both human and divine, who is to me a familiar presence, who dwells with men, not remote and inaccessible, not incarnate in the form of a beast. I pray to him with upright form and uplifted hands, as man to man." And to the Assyrian : "I am a freeman, the slave of no despot ; I reject your splendour for the one, your cowering misery for the many. Your monarch is a tyrant, your boasted magnificence is barbarism." And to both he said as an artist : "Your art is monotonous and lifeless, because it is priest- and tyrant-ridden, because the individual artist is nothing, the precept he inculcates everything. Your history, that should live and breathe upon your sculptured walls, is a bare chronicle. Your gods are not persons but attributes: you tolerate the ugly for the sake of dogma. You are a nation of symbols, of abstractions, of fantastic speculation. In religion as in art, at one moment licentious, at another you are rigidly didactic. Because you disallow reason you are forced to be chimerical."

This profession of faith was not put into words, but we read it in Greek history. The drift of things was not perceived in a day. For a time Greece yielded in part to the dazzling temptation; to the end her handicraftsmen, as opposed to her true artists, adopted a system of ornamentation from the East. Hundreds of vases of all periods, embodying some chance oriental conception, rise up to witness to the fact. A Pegasus, a Chimaera, a Sphinx, a Siren, survive to tell the story of oriental influence. But such instances are comparatively few and scattered. They remain, it has been well said, as foreign words borrowed into a language, but never wholly naturalised. The seventh and the sixth century B.C. witnessed the struggle in which Greece came out victorious. We see the victory even in the rude naturalism of the Heracles of Selinus; the grinning Medusa has already lost something of her oriental formalism. As in matters intellectual Greece loosed her bands, and with happy and gracious flexibility entered on untried courses, so in art, too, there was emancipation. No longer is it sign upon sign and symbol upon symbol. The early Greeks look in wonder at their own plastic or sculptured creations and fancy them to be things of life. "In their hearts," says Homer of the golden handmaids of Hephaestus, "they have understanding, they have also voice and strength, and from the immortal gods they have skill in handicraft."[1] No longer are the arms welded to the sides, the eyelids fastened over the eyeballs, and the whole form fixed immovably to a chair. The images of Daedalus, who was the mythical author of this change, are said to have been tied by chains, lest they should "walk off like runaway slaves."[2]

This brief sketch may serve to indicate the sense in which Greek art unites in itself the qualities most distinctive of the Greek genius,—the love of knowledge, the love of rational beauty, the love of freedom. In their first contact with the East—with Egypt and Assyria—during the period known as the Graeco-Phoenician period

[1] *Iliad* xviii. 419-20. [2] Plato, *Meno* 159 D.

of art, the Greeks had a trying ordeal to pass through. They came out of it, as we have seen, in a characteristic fashion.

1. Their political instinct was alien to Assyrian despotism.

2. Their lay instinct rose up against Egyptian priestcraft.

3. Their instinct for beauty and reason combined rejected in both arts — in Assyrian and Egyptian alike—what was monstrous and lifeless.

4. Their instinct for knowledge, their curiosity, their cosmopolitanism, led them to adopt the foreign *technique*, and to absorb all that was fruitful in the foreigners' ideas. They borrowed from every source, but all that they borrowed they made their own. The Phoenicians, it has been said, taught the Greeks writing, but it was the Greeks who wrote. In every department the principle holds good. They stamped their genius upon each imported product, which was to them but the raw material of their art.

It was not till after the Persian invasion that Greece, which had now and again shown signs of backsliding, severed itself decisively from the East. The barbarian, as if to make place for the new order, had in his reckless havoc swept away the artistic landmarks of the old. The dwelling-place of the earth-born Erechtheus lay in ruins. The ancient temple of Athene Polias was dismantled. Such cults as these, local, narrow, hieratic, could no longer satisfy the aspirations of the victorious people. They needed a worship that should do more than glorify their god, one that should give utterance to themselves. It became with them a national passion to find artistic expression for their sense of deliverance, to write for all time upon Pentelic marble the story of the triumph of light over darkness, of West over East. The triumph had been pan-Hellenic, their worship henceforth must be pan-Olympian. In the new temple of Athene Polias, with her new title of Parthenos, this story took shape. No stone of the fabric but tells the tale. In the eastern pediment is sculptured the first act of the drama, the first note of the people's triumph, the birth of the goddess as virgin, her kinship as Olympian. At the dawn the horses of Helios are uprising, and the chariot of Selene, the moon-goddess, sinks into the sea; for Athene is born, the Olympian, and the shadows melt from before her. She is born not of the earth but of the very brain of Zeus, with all the cosmic circumstance of sea and land

and sun and moon. In the western pediment the second act is rehearsed, the rivalry of Athene and Poseidon,—which of these two with the better gift shall dower the land. Poseidon brings his goodly horses and the sea's dominion, but Athene's gift is preferred—the sea-green olive, "unconquered, self-renewing."[1] In the sculptured metopes that adorn the Doric frieze the contrast, nay, the conflict is more clearly expressed. The Lapith ancestor of many a noble Athenian, the law-abiding Greek, contends with the monstrous Centaur, the man-horse, the type of barbarian licence in the Gigantomachia. The whole phalanx of the Olympians is set in battle array against the earth-born and rebel giants. The heroes of Athens prevail here over the lawless womenfolk of the Amazons, there over the beleaguered city of half-oriental Troy. The achievement of mythical ancestors is invested with new meaning, and takes fresh lustre from the late victory over Persia. And if pediment and metope tell of the remote past, the splendour of the present is unfolded in the frieze of the cella. The body-politic of Athens in its new-found triumph and freedom is here enrolled in sculptured procession —young men, princely and proud, "slaves of no

[1] Soph. *O. C.* 698, φύτευμ' ἀχείρωτον αὐτοποιόν.

man, servants of none"; maidens bearing aloft the sacred vessels, without sign of shame upon their brows. Here we have no sin-laden devotees making expiation, but godlike men worshipping their human gods, gods who sit in easy fellowship awaiting the homage of those who are almost their peers. The spirit of the worshippers reflects the spirit of the goddess; they are reasonable, fearless, temperate.

Yet in this new outburst of life, this self-conscious expression of freedom, the past is not lightly set aside. Though in the centre of the western pediment the two Olympians contend to do the city honour, it is the ancient heroes and gods of the land who adjudge the strife. Cecrops is still there with his faithful daughter, and in the pediment angle recline the two local river-gods. Though a splendid image of gold and ivory was upreared to Athene Polias in her new aspect of Parthenos, the ancient heaven-descended image was not forgotten. Another Erechtheum was raised to be the home of venerable cults; within its precincts were sheltered the sacred serpent, the olive-tree, the trident mark, the ancient leaf-covered Hermes, the altars of half-forgotten priest-kings, the Butadae. Now, for a moment at least, Athens, at this happy pause in her career, unites a reverent conservatism with her forward and inquiring temper. Art, science, religion, have balanced their several claims. Science stays her encroachments, and is not wise over-much.

Such, briefly, is our debt to Greece. And when we speak of Greece we think first of Athens. To Greece herself Athens seemed to offer a perpetual *πανήγυρις*,[1] a feast of language and of thought to which all were welcome who shared in the spirit of the Hellenic brotherhood. To citizens and to strangers by means of epic recitations and dramatic spectacles she presented an idealised image of life itself. She was the home of new ideas, the mother-city from which poetry, eloquence, and philosophy spread to distant lands. While the chief dialects of Greece survive, each not as a mere dialect but as the language of literature—a thing unknown in the history of any other people—the Attic idiom, in which the characteristic elements of other dialects met and were harmonised, has become to us, as it did to the ancients, the very type of Hellenic speech. Athens was not only the "capital of

[1] Isocr. *Panegyr.* § 46.

Greece,"[1] the "school of Greece";[2] it deserves the name applied to it in an epitaph on Euripides: "his country is Athens, *Greece of Greece*."[3] The rays of the Greek genius here found a centre and a focus.

To Greece, then, we owe the love of Science, the love of Art, the love of Freedom: not Science alone, Art alone, or Freedom alone, but these vitally correlated with one another and brought into organic union. And in this union we recognise the distinctive features of the West. The Greek genius is the European genius in its first and brightest bloom. From a vivifying contact with the Greek spirit Europe derived that new and mighty impulse which we call progress. Strange it is to think that these Greeks, like the other members of the Indo-European family, probably had their cradle in the East; that behind Greek civilisation, Greek language, Greek mythology, there is that Eastern background to which the comparative sciences seem to point. But it is no more than a background. In spite of all resemblances, in spite of common customs,

[1] Isocr. *Antid.* § 299, ἄστυ τῆς Ἑλλάδος.

[2] Thucyd. ii. 41, τῆς Ἑλλάδος παίδευσιν.

[3] *Anth. Pal.* vii. 45, πατρὶς δ' Ἑλλάδος Ἑλλὰς Ἀθῆναι.

common words, common syntax, common gods, the spirit of the Greeks and of their Eastern kinsmen — the spirit of their civilisation, art, language, and mythology — remains essentially distinct. The Greeks, when first they meet us in history, fancy themselves to have been born on the soil; they have no memory of their Asiatic origin. They were blest with the faculty of *forgetting* — one of the happiest gifts a nation can possess. And their own sense of difference and distinction was at bottom true. The Greek genius, with its potent originality, had transformed, if not effaced, the Eastern features. The Greek victories over the East at Marathon and Salamis were but the earnest of a victory that had been long preparing for the Western world. Much yet remained to be done by Rome, and much by the Teutonic nations, for Greece left many blots and flaws in her political and social system. But the broad lines had been already traced along which there was to be forward movement.

From Greece came that first mighty impulse whose far-off workings are felt by us to-day, and which has brought it about that progress has been accepted as the law and goal of human endeavour. Greece first took up the task of equipping man with all that fits him for civil life and promotes his secular wellbeing; of unfolding and expanding every inborn faculty and energy, bodily and mental; of striving restlessly after the perfection of the whole, and finding in this effort after an unattainable ideal that by which man becomes like to the gods. The life of the Hellenes, like that of their epic hero Achilles, was brief and brilliant. But they have been endowed with the gift of renewing their youth. Renan, speaking of the nations that are fitted to play a part in universal history, says "that they must die first that the world may live through them"; that "a people must choose between the prolonged life, the tranquil and obscure destiny of one who lives for himself; and the troubled, stormy career of one who lives for humanity. The nation which revolves within its breast social and religious problems is always weak politically. Thus it was with the Jews, who in order to make the religious conquest of the world must needs disappear as a nation."[1] "They lost a material city, they opened the reign of the spiritual Jerusalem." So too it was with Greece. As a people she ceased to be. When her freedom was overthrown at Chaeronea,

[1] *Conférences d'Angleterre*, p. 103.

the page of her history was to all appearance closed. Yet from that moment she was to enter on a larger life and on universal empire. Already, during the last days of her independence it had been possible to speak of a new Hellenism, which rested not on ties of blood but on spiritual kinship. This presentiment of Isocrates was marvellously realised. As Alexander passed conquering through Asia, he restored to the East, as garnered grain, that Greek civilisation whose seeds had long ago been received from the East. Each conqueror in turn, the Macedonian and the Roman, bowed before conquered Greece and learnt lessons at her feet. To the modern world too Greece has been the great civiliser, the ecumenical teacher, the disturber and regenerator of slumbering societies. She is the source of most of the quickening ideas which re-make nations and renovate literature and art. If we reckon up our secular possessions, the wealth and heritage of the past, the larger share may be traced back to Greece. One half of life she has made her domain—all, or well-nigh all, that belongs to the present order of things and to the visible world.

"We are all Greeks," says Shelley; "our laws, our literature, our religion, our art, have their roots in Greece." This is somewhat overstated: neither our laws, nor our religion are derived from Greece. Our religion has come to us from the East, though it too has been breathed upon and, in a sense, transformed by the Western spirit. Greek polytheism was doomed to sterility, on the side both of speculation and of conduct. Though the poets of Greece, like the Hebrew prophets, tried to ennoble the popular religion; though Pindar, Aeschylus, and Sophocles, by a purifying and reflective process, imported into polytheism lofty religious conceptions and a grave ideal of conduct, yet polytheism could not bear the strain. It could not receive within it the new content. The philosophers were more ruthless and clear-sighted than the poets. From the beginning, philosophy made war on polytheism; it aimed not at reform, but at destruction.

The tide of conquest was rolled back, and our religion has come to us from the East,—but from an East how different from that out of which Greece emerged, or from that which she vanquished at Salamis! In those earlier ages, the victory of the East over Greece would have been the triumph of nature over man, of necessity over moral freedom, of a caste system or of despotism over free organisation and intelligence, of stagnation over progress, of symbolism over beauty, of the arid plain over the mountain and the sea. The actual victory of East over West which took place at the triumph of Christianity, had in it no such sinister meaning. Greece had already won freedom in all its branches —freedom for society, freedom for the individual, freedom for thought. She had written her spirit in books and on tables of stone, which time has spared for our reading, and which record the supremacy of mind over sense, of spirit over matter. She had shown how the love of beauty might be united with the love of truth, art with science, how reason might be made imaginative. She had given living history for dry chronicle, oratory for rhetoric, sober imagination for Eastern phantasy. This imperishable legacy she left to mankind. She could now afford to give place to an Eastern religion. Henceforth it is in the confluence of the Hellenic stream of thought with the waters that flow from Hebrew sources that the main direction of the world's progress is to be sought. The two tendencies summed up in the world's Hebraism and Hellenism are often regarded as opposing and irreconcilable forces ; and, indeed, it is only in a few rarely gifted individuals that these principles have been perfectly harmonised. Yet harmonised they can and must be. How to do so is one of the problems of modern civilisation ;—how we are to unite the dominant Hebrew idea of a divine law of righteousness and of a supreme spiritual faculty with the Hellenic conception of human energies, manifold and expansive, each of which claims for itself unimpeded play ; how life may gain unity without incurring the reproach of onesidedness ; how, in a word, Religion may be combined with Culture.

THE GREEK IDEA OF THE STATE

THE prevailing conception of the State in our own day is that of a vast mechanism for controlling and regulating the action of Society. It is a whole made up of government departments, an army of officials, headed by the policeman and the tax-collector, all set in motion by a supreme legislature. To some minds it presents itself as a hostile force, thwarting our natural impulses and imposing checks upon individual freedom. Yet it cannot be dispensed with altogether, for without it Society would go to pieces. None the less it is an evil. Its action must be restricted to the utmost,—some would say limited to the protection of life and property and to ensuring the fulfilment of legal engagements. For these purposes it must be armed with the authority of the nation. Individuals surrender something, but in return get more than they give up. Beyond this point the well-intentioned but clumsy efforts of the State to make men good and to make them wise fare no better than those of the individual busybody who in season and out of season concerns himself with his neighbour's welfare, and reforms him against his will. As for the higher mental faculties they are withered and paralysed under the shadow of State patronage. According to this view the State is always meddling, always encroaching ; it is trying to do everybody's work and does it all badly. Others, still regarding the State as a great machinery, hold that the machinery is only half utilised, that much beneficent action is arrested simply because the State refrains from touching the proper springs. Or, it is said that the works are antiquated, and that State action will only be effectual when the machinery of State is renewed. In either case stress is laid on the ubiquitous and penetrating influence of the State, on the vast forces at its disposal, greater than any individuals or association of individuals can ever wield. The State in this view ought to undertake ampler duties—nothing less than the general task of social regeneration. To this end it must reorganise the whole industrial and economic system, and marshal men in new groups and combinations, assigning to each its special function. It will minister to the souls as well as to the bodies of its citizens. By salutary restrictions it will withdraw the facilities for vice, and by raising the standard of material prosperity it will remove many existing temptations.

These are two extreme views between which there are various tenable positions. They are held by thinkers, they are in the minds of ordinary men. But that which is common to all such views is the conception of the State as distinct from Society, taking upon itself the business of Society, acting on its behalf, with more or less success or bungling as the case may be. The State is a thing external to the individual citizen, administering his affairs, claiming his obedience, prescribing certain acts, forbidding others. Though the citizen himself, under a system of popular institutions, is the ultimate source of the authority of the State, yet in large States he hardly recognises as his own the delegated rule. He has officials to act for him in all the details of government. They hold, as it were, the seals of State. The sovereign people abdicates office and only at intervals resumes the reins of power, and reminds itself of its rights by signing voting papers. At shorter intervals it may perhaps issue certain intermediate orders—direct mandates to its representatives, whom it is apt to relieve of the task of thinking for themselves. But all the hard work, the everyday business of administration, it leaves to be done by officials—either by permanent officials, the silent men who do not talk but work, or by elective Boards, much of whose work consists in talking. The private citizen, who holds no official position, almost forgets except at election times that he has a share in governing as well as in being governed. The call that occasionally comes to him in this country to serve as a juror is an unwelcome reminder that he is himself a vital part of the organisation of government.

The severance of the ordinary citizen from the active business of the State, as distinct from the function of talking or voting, is rendered almost necessary by the dimensions to which the modern State has grown. From the City of the ancient world it has expanded into the Nation ; it numbers its millions where in old days there were thousands, men who are connected together by links and relations of ever-increasing complexity. In some countries the detachment I speak of is less complete than in others ; for local government, when based on rational principles, can do something towards restoring the unity of the body corporate. But to the great majority of citizens the State is an inherited system or organisation, an abstraction that is outside themselves; or else, when it acts in its collective capacity and as an individual, it comes to be identified with the Executive, that is, with the Government of the day: in which case it is to one half of the community no longer even a harmless abstraction, but consists of a band of political opponents whom the other party are accustomed in their speech, if not in their hearts, to regard as the enemies of the country. The idea of the State suffers grievously from being thought of, at the best, as a machinery of government, at the worst, as a party organisation. With such associations no emotion or living sentiment can gather round it. The cause of Country is one for which men will now, as of old, do great deeds and sacrifice all. The interests of the State seem a thing apart. There is no spell about the word. The State, people say, is well able to take care of itself.

All this forms a striking contrast with the idea which, for a brief and fortunate moment in the history of the world, prevailed in Greece. To the common consciousness of Greece the State or the

City was not an organisation but an organism, no lifeless machine of government, no alien force imposing itself upon the citizen, but a living whole which took up into itself all individual wills: not impeding spontaneous energies or crushing individual growth, but enriching and completing the individualities which it embraced. It was the individual on his ideal side; his true and spiritual self; the glorified expression and embodiment of his noblest aims and faculties; the higher unity in which he merged his separate or selfish self; the enduring substance which outlived his transient existence. From it were derived and back into it flowed all the currents of individual life. "The Man *versus* the State" was a phrase unknown; the Man was complete in the State; apart from it he was not only incomplete, he had no rational existence. Only through the social organism could each part, by adaptation to the others, develop its inherent powers. To the Greeks Society and the State were one and indivisible. Different constitutions in various degrees approximated to this idea; only under some form of republic, however, could the full conception be realised, for there only could each citizen be said to be at once "ruler and ruled" (ἄρχειν καὶ *ἄρχεσθαι*); a member of Society, and at the same time a member of the Government. At Athens a citizen voted and spoke in the assembly and sat on a jury on one and the same principle as that on which he served in the army. It was no mere right or privilege, but a duty which the State claimed from him in virtue of his citizenship. In one case as in the other he might shirk the duty, but if he did so he failed to fulfil his proper function. Nor was it at Athens only that this idea prevailed. In a fragment of Democritus, the philosopher of Abdera, we find it said, that the neglect of public business wins a man a bad name, though he may not be guilty of thieving or dishonesty.[1] But the fact and the idea soon ceased to correspond. In the fourth century B.C. the sense of estrangement between Society and the State had made itself felt, and the individual, absorbed in separate interests, withdrew from the service of the commonwealth. The Greek State in its distinctive form and true idea was then approaching its end. It was one of the fatal signs and warnings of decay. The unity of Greek life could not survive the growth of a conscious individualism.

[1] Democr. Fr. 213.

We sometimes forget how memorable, how original a creation the Greek State was—hardly less striking in its originality than the creations of Greece in art, philosophy, and literature, or than her discoveries in the region of pure science. We think less of it than it deserves because it had not, and in the nature of things could not have, the same stamp of permanence, of universality, of final achievement, that belongs to those other products of the Greek genius. But let us look for a moment at the place it holds in universal history.

In the pre-Grecian world the State and the Individual had stood apart. There had been despotism and there had been anarchy. Society had oscillated between these two poles, the rule of the one man in a world of slaves, and the license of a multitude who could not be called free because they obeyed only their own caprice. The two principles had confronted one another as irreconcilable opposites. Like any other abstract principle when left to work itself out alone, each of these ideas led to fanaticism. It seemed as if Society must ever consume itself in inward strife or drag out a torpid existence. Greece offered the first solution of the antithesis of

Freedom and Necessity in the domain of politics, a solution far from final, yet an immeasurable advance upon all that had been done before: for it introduced into politics a principle of mediation, of rational compromise, which has ever since been among the most potent instruments of progress.

For the Greek state had in it that which made it akin at once to a natural unity and to a voluntary union. It rested on definite and enduring relations which were above the caprice of the individual; the citizen entered at birth into the common heritage of race, language, and religion; he found about him a framework of customs and institutions which he had not made and as little could unmake. On the other hand, he felt no revolt against these fixed conditions of his civic existence. Within the sphere of City life he moved as in his native element. He was aware indeed of newly awakened faculties and of his own independent existence in the community, but unconscious as yet of antagonism as well as difference. Each citizen was vitally one with all the rest—one with the social organism and with his whole environment. With the awakening of this conscious life, Reason as a self-determining and organising force had entered into secular society. Reason too had its conflicts; it worked in the stormy atmosphere of political debate; in the blind struggles of parties and factions which almost rent the State in twain. Yet once heard it could not be silenced. In free and fierce discussion it matured its powers; tyranny and anarchy gave way before it; and it was the triumph of Greece not only that it produced immortal writers and immortal artists, but that it gave to human society a new starting-point and a new direction. Instead of obedience to a despotic will, or the unending conflict of individual passions, it established Reason as the arbiter and guide of civic life—Reason or λόγος in its twofold supremacy as Rational Thought and Rational Speech.

This Reason, as the principle which inspired the social organism, was embodied in Law. Law to the Greeks is Reason made articulate, the public conscience of the community finding for itself expression. In its severe impartiality it is free from human prejudice and passion; it is *νοῦς ἄνευ ὀρέξεως*[1]—"Reason without desire." It has on the one hand an *ἀναγκαστικὴ δύναμις*,[2] a com-

[1] Arist. *Pol.* iii. 16. 1287 a 32.

[2] Arist. *Eth. Nic.* x. 10. 1180 a 21.

pelling power more constraining than a parent's authority. Yet the constraint is a voluntary one, it is the moral compulsion or *ἀνάγκη* which only freemen can impose upon themselves. Hence in Greek literature Law has another side than that of an impersonal authority that claims allegiance. It speaks in two voices, in a voice of stern compulsion and in accents of reasonable persuasion. To each citizen it addresses itself as his own *alter ego*, his best, his higher self. In Plato's *Crito* the Laws are made to present themselves in person to Socrates in prison not only as the guardians of his liberty but as his lifelong friends, his well-wishers, his equals, with whom he had of his own free-will entered into binding compact. Elsewhere[1] Plato puts aside the thought of the Laws as "tyrants and masters who command and threaten, and after writing their decrees on walls go their ways." Rather do they reason with men and seek to win their intelligent consent, and only in the last resort do they threaten pains and penalties. In the same context the exhortation of the Laws is compared to that of the poets and of those writers "who in metre or out of metre

[1] Plat. *Laws* ix. 859 A, κατὰ τύραννον καὶ δεσπότην, τάξαντα καὶ ἀπειλήσαντα, γράψαντα ἐν τοίχοις ἀπηλλάχθαι.

have recorded their notes for the guidance of life."[1]

In entire accordance too with the sentiment of Greece, Plato[2] recognises a region between admonition and positive law over which the lawgiver has control. Part of the office of the lawgiver[3] was to be a moral teacher, a preacher of righteousness; to prescribe the acts that ought to be done and also to reveal and to inspire in men the true motives of action; to create a disposition no less than to enforce outward conformity; to work into the complex web of national life all the influences that may ennoble and enrich it. To the great lawgivers of the past the Greeks looked back as other nations do to the founders or reformers of their religion. They were the inspired men who had been the salvation of their States. Law as promulgated by them was not a code of prohibitions nor was it limited to the corrective justice of the law-courts. Its range was wider than that of morality itself. Institutions, in the eyes of the Greeks, were the

[1] Plat. *Laws* ix. 858 D, *ὅσοι ἄνευ μέτρων καὶ μετὰ μέτρων τὴν αὑτῶν εἰς μνήμην ξυμβουλὴν περὶ βίου κατέθεντο συγγράψαντες.*

[2] *Ib.* vii. 822, 823.

[3] Here and in much of what follows I am under deep obligations to W. L. Newman's *Politics of Aristotle*, vol. i.

creations of Law. Traditions and customs rested on its sanction. Ideals of conduct, types of national character, were moulded by its influence. The inspirations of heroism were traced to it as their source. Law blended with religion, morality, and public opinion, and by its subtle operation subdued society to its will. It was invested with spiritual efficacy and power. The Law of the Greeks was at once the Law and the Prophets of the Hebrews.

It is easy here to see how much that was really due to national history and character, to religion, to the force of circumstances, to the silent impact and pressure of society on the individual, was put down to the direct action of Law or of the lawgiver. And it is equally clear that the conception of Law here indicated was not one on which a great fabric of jurisprudence could be reared. For that we must look elsewhere. But it is a point of view which presents features of unique interest. We have Law not as in Judaism, a system of rigid rules, a bondage to external ordinances, "touch not, taste not, handle not"; not as in Rome a code of abstract rights, resting on a doctrine of legal personality; but Law as the organ and collective voice of freemen and fellow-citizens, more sacred, more binding upon the conscience than any external commands; Law as a divine element immanent in human nature, Reason made animate and pleading with men in accents of emotion. Well might the orators declare that democracy in its true idea was the reign of Law. And, indeed, Aristotle notes that the worst fault of an extreme or untempered democracy is its lawlessness,—that is, the reign of arbitrary will, the negation of Hellenic freedom. When each man does what is good in his own eyes, reason is dethroned and passing impulse takes its place. "But this is all wrong; men should not think it slavery to live according to the rule of the constitution, for it is their salvation."[1] The service of the laws, says Plato, is also the service of the gods—a service in which to obey is nobler than to rule.[2]

The first great advance, then, made by the Greeks in determining the relations of the State and the Individual consisted in the voluntary subordination of the individual will to the will of

[1] Arist. *Pol.* viii. (v.) 9. 1310 a 34, τοῦτο δ' ἐστὶ φαῦλον· οὐ γὰρ δεῖ οἴεσθαι δουλείαν εἶναι τὸ ζῆν πρὸς τὴν πολιτείαν, ἀλλὰ σωτηρίαν.

[2] Plat. *Laws* vi. 762 E, καλλωπίζεσθαι χρὴ τῷ καλῶς δουλεῦσαι μᾶλλον ἢ τῷ καλῶς ἄρξαι, πρῶτον μὲν τοῖς νόμοις, ὡς ταύτην τοῖς θεοῖς οὖσαν δουλείαν, ἔπειτα κ.τ.λ.

the community. In this act of self-surrender the citizen realised his true self, he became conscious of spiritual freedom. When Demosthenes[1] passionately calls upon the Athenians to "belong to themselves," "to become their own masters," "to assert their freedom," he says not a different thing from Aristotle, but the same thing as when Aristotle declares[2] that "no citizen belongs to himself but that all belong to the State." What Demosthenes desires is an emancipation from selfish aims, from flattering counsellors, an assertion of the true and corporate self, as exhibited in an entire devotion to the public good. Absolute self-sacrifice for the interests of the State, personal service for the country—this he meant by freedom. He would restore the old ideal of Athenian character which we read of in Thucydides:[3] "Their bodies they devote to their country, as though they belonged to other men; their true self is their mind which is most truly their own when employed in her service."

[1] Dem. *Phil.* i. 7, ἐὰν ὑμῶν αὐτῶν ἐθελήσητε γενέσθαι. So *Olynth.* ii. 30.

[2] Arist. *Pol.* v. (viii.) I. 1337 a 27, οὐδὲ χρὴ νομίζειν αὐτὸν αὑτοῦ τινα εἶναι τῶν πολιτῶν, ἀλλὰ πάντας τῆς πόλεως.

[3] Thucyd. i. 70, 6 (Jowett's Translation), ἔτι δὲ τοῖς μὲν σώμασιν ἀλλοτριωτάτοις ὑπὲρ τῆς πόλεως χρῶνται, τῇ γνώμῃ δὲ οἰκειοτάτῃ ἐς τὸ πράσσειν τὰ ὑπὲρ αὐτῆς.

The *Politics* of Aristotle more than any other single book gives an orderly and comprehensive notion of what the Greeks meant by the State. There, as in the *Ethics*, Aristotle embodies for us the common sense of Greece; raised, however, as it were, to a higher power, clarified and systematised in passing through a master-mind. The picture of the State as it ought to be is, indeed, far enough removed in its details from the State as it was. Yet Aristotle is faithful to the principles that inspired Greek life. His ideal is not an arbitrary creation, a work of fancy. It stands in much closer relation to the reality than the *Republic* of Plato; for though he, like Plato, sees the need of reconstruction for society, he does not break so sharply with the past. He had profoundly studied all existing political constitutions; he had surveyed Hellenic civilisation in all its phases. In the *Politics* he gathers up the experience of the past; he takes account of all current conceptions and actual institutions; he recombines in a larger view popular opinions and lifts them into a higher plane of thought.

The State, then, as he describes it, is not an association for the protection of rights and nothing more. Such a view had been put forward by the

Sophist Lycophron,[1] and was afterwards held by the Epicureans. It gained acceptance in the decline of Greek life, and was itself a symptom of the decline. It belonged to an age when the individual, severed from the State, claimed for himself prior rights, and looked to the State only as a means of securing for himself peace of mind and personal independence. Nor, again, does the State exist for the increase of wealth, for the development of trade, or for the extension of empire. The State, according to Aristotle, is a union or brotherhood of equal men, who are able and purposed to rule and to be ruled; not brought together by force or fear, but animated by a single aim—to live the noblest life of which men are capable, in the unimpeded exercise of the highest qualities, moral and intellectual. The State exists not for the sake of "life," but of a "good life"—(not *τοῦ ζῆν* but *τοῦ εὖ ζῆν ἕνεκα*)—which is the end of man. Certain external means of life are necessary and presupposed, for without them the play of the faculties would be impeded. But the conditions of life must not be confounded with the end of life. Some persons by reason of age or

[1] *Polit.* iii. 9. 1280 b 10, *ὁ νόμος συνθήκη καί, καθάπερ ἔφη Λυκόφρων ὁ σοφιστής, ἐγγυητὴς ἀλλήλοις τῶν δικαίων.*

sex or race or disqualifying occupations were, according to Aristotle, cut off from any true participation in the life of the State. They could not become organic parts of the community, but were fitted only for lower and ministerial functions. Those only were capable of membership who could live for noble ends; whose souls and bodies were not by nature incomplete and inadequate to the great demands that were to be made on them, or marred by sordid or engrossing occupations. Aristotle, in excluding from citizenship certain classes other than slaves on the ground that their employments were degrading, departs from the accepted usages of Greece. He is, however, merely exaggerating a feeling of contempt that was entertained for manual and industrial labour almost everywhere except, perhaps, at Athens.

In the broad lines of his teaching Aristotle, as we have said, falls in with the educated opinion and the traditions of Greece; but these he deepens and enlarges. The State, for him, has a spiritual function. It does not exist for the satisfaction of bodily and material wants. Such wants it must supply, but its true aim lies beyond. It must look to the higher and spiritual needs of society. It must build up character and intellect. It must content itself with no one-sided type. It must unfold all the powers of the individual. It must train up its citizens to the full stature of the perfect man. It must promote not virtue alone but virtuous action, virtue flowing over into a life of moral and mental activity. *Πόλις ἄνδρα διδάσκει* was a saying of Simonides. The City was the teacher, the guide of life, the sovereign educator. The truth of this had been felt and acted on in Greece. Each City stood out as a person, a moral agent. It had its own character (*ἦθος*) and individual stamp. That character it impressed upon its members. Manifold were the agencies and influences by which it worked. It spoke to the citizens through its laws and constitution,[1] which were the truest image of itself. It spoke, as at Athens, through its art and architecture, in which the service of the State and of religion was united. It spoke through the poets, who at the great public festivals were more than private individuals. They bore, in some sort, the commission of the State; and, when in the hearing of their fellow-citizens they set forth their deepest thoughts upon

[1] Cp. Plato, *Ep.* v. 321, ἔστι γὰρ δή τις φωνὴ τῶν πολιτειῶν ἑκάστης, καθαπερεὶ τινῶν ζῴων, ἄλλη μὲν δημοκρατίας ἄλλη δ' ὀλιγαρχίας ἡ δ' αὖ μοναρχίας.

the problems of life, they did their part towards harmonising ancient pieties and sacred legend with the moral sense of a more reflective age.

All this the State had done. But it might do yet more. So at least thought both Plato and Aristotle. It might directly take on itself the spiritual leadership of society. Formerly men had looked to Delphi to carry out this work. It was no mere curiosity about the future that impelled the Greeks to inquire of Apollo. The questions which they addressed to the god concerned not only the changing fortunes of individuals or nations but the ordinances of divine law and the conduct of life. The purpose of the Delphic religion was to bear testimony to the eternal moral principles of which the gods were guardians, and to bring men into harmony with the divine will. As the god of purity, Apollo demanded not only outward ceremonial but purity of heart. As Μουσαγέτης, he was the god of art, of science, and of poetry, and aspired to organise the civic and national life. From the sanctuary at Delphi rules went forth for the discipline of states, for the shaping of law and custom, for the planting of colonies on every shore to which Greek seamen had penetrated. The influence of Delphi was in no small measure akin to that of Hebrew prophecy. The many-sided culture, artistic and intellectual, which proceeded from Delphi had indeed no counterpart among the Jews; yet the Hebrew prophet, one part of whose office was to rehearse the history of Israel, to comment on the disasters and deliverances of the nation and to interpret past experience, exercised a function not unlike that of Delphi. In each institution, too, there was an assertion of the spirit over the letter; in each the written law received a new and similar interpretation. "Clean hands and a pure heart" were required of all who would approach the holy hill either of Zion or of Parnassus. The conception of religion was transformed when it was detached from merely ritual practices and made to consist in the disposition of the mind and soul. When in Greek writers of the fourth century B.C. we come across such expressions as this,—that justice and goodness are the best of sacrifices, and prevail with the gods more than a hecatomb of victims,[1] we hear the echo of the teaching of Delphi. The idea is the same as was proclaimed in the words of the prophet: "To what purpose is the multitude of your sacrifices? . . . Bring me

[1] Isoc. *Nicocles* § 20. Cp. Plat. *Laws* iv. 716 D.

no more vain oblations. . . . Wash you, make you clean; put away the evil of your doings from before mine eyes; cease to do evil; learn to do well."

Delphi proved false to the trust that had been committed to her. The desire of wealth and power was her ruin. Enriched by offerings of pilgrims, by fines and confiscations, by the levy of tithes, she was drawn into the arena of political conflict. Nor could she hold herself aloof from party intrigues in the various states which looked to her for guidance. It was not, however, till the Persian wars that she finally forfeited her place, and renounced her right to represent Greek nationality and the ideal sentiment of the people. In aspiring to secular and material power she lost her spiritual dominion. Her influence did not at once die out. It perpetuates itself in other forms throughout Greek history and literature. We meet it not only in the lyrics of Pindar, but in the lives and works of the men who are most Hellenic among the Hellenes—in the poetry of Aeschylus and Sophocles, in the art of Phidias, in the philosophy of Plato, in the lives of Socrates, Epaminondas, Demosthenes, Callicratidas. But the integrity of Delphi itself was lost; and in the fourth century B.C. the Greek world lacked a religious centre, and craved for some authoritative voice in conduct and belief.

Society stood in deep need of moral guidance and regeneration. The foundations of right and wrong, of public and private morality, had been questioned. The states of Greece were cut in two by faction. The members of a political party were a sworn brotherhood—Aristotle preserves for us one of the forms of the oligarchical oath[1]—pledged not only to be loyal to one another, but to do their opponents all the harm of which they were capable. Where, then, was a power which could restore unity and could rest morality once more on a sure basis? All Greek tradition pointed to the State. It alone seemed capable of the task. Alone it could speak with authority and had coercive force behind it. On the State, accordingly, Plato and Aristotle devolve many of the functions which were afterwards peculiar to the Christian Church. To the ancient world it never occurred that the State was "profane," nor would the distinction between Church and State have been intelligible to the Greeks. Religious worship and ritual were inwrought into

[1] Arist. *Pol.* viii. (v.) 9. 1310 a 9, *καὶ τῷ δήμῳ κακόνους ἔσομαι καὶ βουλεύσω ὅ τι ἂν ἔχω κακόν.*

the texture of their political and social life. The Greek city was invested with a sacred character from the outset; it was the chosen home of protecting gods, the embodiment of the moral law, the visible expression of those ideal interests which were symbolised by the popular religion. Hence it was no startling innovation to regard each City as a spiritual centre for its own citizens, an authoritative exponent in matters of conscience and conduct.

But the State, as conceived by the philosophers, while in one aspect it resembled a Church, was also something more than a Church. On its secular side statesmanship had to concern itself with the outward means of livelihood, to regulate the production and distribution of wealth; to lay down minute rules for the guidance of the individual from the cradle to the grave; to exercise supreme control over all the practical arts, assigning to each its due rank and place.[1] It had to prescribe what sciences should be admitted and studied by different classes within the community. Above all the complete culture and education of the citizen must be undertaken by the State; for this, the highest of all civic interests, was under

[1] Arist. *Eth. Nic.* i. 1. 1094 a 27 *sqq.*

existing social arrangements most defective. It must no longer be left in private hands, as at Athens. The training of the citizen thus becomes the chief concern of the political philosopher. Severe indeed was the preparation and long and arduous the self-discipline enjoined upon those who were to be rulers in the State; and if few could hope to attain to such perfection, those few were the men whom nature had marked out as fitted to bear rule. With Aristotle as with Plato the construction of an ideal state merges in a scheme of national education.

We may note in passing certain obvious defects in the general view of the State which we have been considering. The State is intended to wield an unlimited sway for which it is unfitted. Its control over the individual, extending to the details of domestic life and to thought as well as action, could not but defeat the purposes of culture and free self-development which it was intended to promote. The vexatious rules and restrictions of the ideal commonwealths outnumber those of the actual Greek States. These were already numerous enough. The individual freedom enjoyed at Athens and extolled by Pericles was plainly an exception to the common usage of

Greece, and is so regarded in the Funeral Speech. The word "freedom," it should be remembered, bore an ambiguous meaning. It denoted on the one hand political independence—the exercise of sovereign power by the State and of political rights by the citizens. In this sense every Greek citizen could claim it as his birthright. Even the Spartans could tell the Persian Hydarnes that he had not, like them, tasted of freedom, and did not know whether it was sweet or not.[1] But the word also denoted personal and social liberty—freedom from the excessive restraints of law, the absence of a tyrannous public opinion and of intolerance between man and man. Pericles claims for Athens "freedom" in this double sense. But freedom so far as it implies the absence of legal interference in the private concerns of life was but little known except at Athens. Even where the individual was not conscious of being subject to irksome regulations and did not chafe under them, yet, as we can now see, the State strained its prerogative and exceeded the limits within which its control could be beneficial. The State as sketched by Plato in the *Republic* and in the *Laws* and by Aristotle in the *Politics* is modelled largely on the

[1] Herod. vii. 135.

constitutions of Sparta and Crete, and exhibits their defects in an extreme form.

Again, in these imaginary commonwealths as in the real states of Greece, a whole class, or even classes, of the community are excluded from civic rights. While the idea had been deeply impressed upon the mind of Greece that government is for the good of the governed, and that the State exists for the welfare of all the citizens and not of some, yet the citizens themselves constituted an exclusive and privileged order. In the actual states the slave class existed in order that the citizen body might be free to do its proper duties. The slaves formed no vital part of the city; they were not sharers in its well-being; they were merely instruments or "living tools" which nature had provided. Possessing only a rudimentary reason—so argued the philosophers—and being therefore incapable of acquiring more than a fraction of virtue and happiness, they differed from the freemen as the body differs from the soul or the brute from the man. It was therefore *better* for them to be servile than to be free. Aristotle, as we have seen, places not only slaves but artisans, labourers, shopkeepers, among the excluded classes; for manual and mercantile labour tended, he thought, to make the minds of men unfree and their bodies degraded. He altogether over-estimates the effect of social condition and occupation upon character. He does not remember his own admission that what makes a pursuit noble or ignoble is not the thing done, but the spirit and motive of the action. "I have known," says Burke, "merchants with the sentiments and abilities of great statesmen, and I have seen persons in the rank of statesmen with the conceptions and characters of pedlars." The "noble life," however, which it is the aim of the State to realise is restricted by Aristotle to politics and philosophy, and, it would seem, to certain forms of art. The purpose of the State being, as he held, to develop the highest and most complete life possible for man, he fixes his attention on this to the neglect of another end, on which most modern reformers lay more stress—that of developing in the mass of the people the highest type of life of which *they* are capable. We observe how Aristotle is here the child of his age. The aristocratic sentiment, which never has been stronger than in the ancient democracies, colours all his thinking.

A certain tone of contempt for what is worthy

but commonplace, a certain exclusiveness of mind, pervades Greek literature up to a late date. Uninteresting and obscure goodness was lightly esteemed by the Greeks. They looked to the dignity, the inherent distinction and excellence of a man's personality. The qualities they admired were hardly to be attained without the advantages of birth and leisure. Their virtues were those of the free man, who is master of himself, lord of circumstances, above sordid anxieties, who respects himself and is respected by others. Amiel in his *Journal d'une Vie Intime*, attempting to elucidate the English word "gentleman," "the Shibboleth of England," says: "Between gentlemen, courtesy, equality, social proprieties; below that level, haughtiness, disdain, coldness, indifference. . . . The politeness of a gentleman is not human and general, but quite individual and personal." It would be an injustice to the Greek to attribute to him all the features of this so-called "gentleman," yet we may see a family likeness between the two types. The Greek ideal of the καλὸς κἀγαθός had in it a touch of aristocratic sentiment; it was well fitted for the favoured few, for the gifted, for the noble, for the strong; but it left out of account the disinherited, the fallen, the feeble of the earth.

Here the Greeks present to us the opposite side of the picture to that which is presented by the Jews. The Hebrew prophets, filled with the hope of seeing a reign of universal justice established in the world, are impatient of social inequalities; they speak of "the poor," "the oppressed," as almost identical in sense with the pious and the good. The Greek philosophers would intensify existing inequalities. They are indeed far removed from the stage of thought represented by Theognis, with whom "the good" meant the nobles; but their ideal conception is still that of an aristocracy—an aristocracy, however, of intellect not of birth.

We must not, of course, forget the glimpses and intuitions of humanity which are revealed in Greek authors with increasing clearness. In Homer already there is a reverence for the stranger and the suppliant, a tenderness towards the weak, a chivalrous honour which exacts less than its rights—this and much more that is contained in the untranslatable word *αἰδώς*, in which the moral sentiment of the heroic age finds its most delicate utterance. Later there is the altar to Pity (Ἔλεος) at Athens; the Attic *φιλανθρωπία* or human kindliness—compassion for the oppressed, generosity towards the vanquished, forgiveness of injuries—which is the pride of the poets and orators. There is, again, in Aristotle a new and almost modern feeling about the poor, and special provisions are made for their welfare.[1] But these sentiments were very partial in their scope; they did not exist towards men as such, but towards special classes and individuals. Even when the sympathy appears to be more broadly human, it is not yet a reasoned principle of action, but rather one of the instinctive virtues of a high-born race which would not shame its lineage by anything mean; and like all instincts is liable to be overborne at short notice by some mastering and competing passion. On the other hand, the Jews of the Old Testament, starting though they did from narrow tribal prejudices, acquired a more universal sympathy. They had learned by suffering. They had been outcasts and oppressed. By sharp discipline they had come to know the meaning of patience, of self-abnegation, of faith in the unseen: and hence by right of deeper insight into the moral needs of man it has been their prerogative to be for all succeeding ages the consolers and interpreters of suffering humanity. They

[1] Arist. *Pol.* vii. (vi.) 5. 1320 a 31 *sqq.*; vi. (iv.) 13. 1297 b 6-12; viii. (v.) 8. 1309 a 20-3.

approached more nearly than the Greeks to the Christianity which places perfection not in dignity, nor in personal distinction, but in love.

The insufficient care for individual freedom in Aristotle, and the moral effacement of certain classes of the community, may be traced back to an imperfect conception of human personality. While Aristotle attributed to the State a more complete personality than it really possessed, he did not grasp the depth and meaning of the personality of the individual. Like the other Greeks of his time he did not appreciate the independent worth and dignity of all human beings. Of man in the exercise of his sovereign faculty of pure reason, man akin to the divine and entering well-nigh on immortality through a life of speculative activity, he speaks with a glow and with an eloquence that are rare in his pages.[1] But to the life of morality without philosophy he assigns but a second place; differing indeed there from Plato, who, holding that by moral virtue a man becomes like to God, exhibits a deeper insight than Aristotle into the notion of personality. Those who believe that the distinctive being of a man, his inmost self, resides in his moral personality, and

[1] Arist. *Eth. Nic.* x. 7. 1177 b 19 *sqq.*

that this is a common bond which unites all human beings as such, and gives to each an equal and independent worth, must feel how inadequate was the conception of the Greeks. To them the idea of man was realised in and through the State; the idea, that is, not of man as man, but of man as a citizen, in his visible relations to the world, relations which varied in each case and created differences that almost effaced the unity of personality. Only here and there does Aristotle rise to the conception of man as such:[1] but the phrase stands apart from his general thought; in its context it is meaningless and illogical, nor is it pushed to its conclusions. Man tends to disappear in the distinctions between husbands, wives, children, slaves and masters. Stoicism led the way to the deeper view of human brotherhood which Christianity revealed. Not until man was rescued out of the kingdom of nature and taken up into the commonwealth of God and into personal relations with the Divine Being, could he be more than the member of a social organism, or an instrument for achieving the ends of the State. Then only did a universal morality become possible and the idea of personality receive its full content.

[1] Arist. *Eth. Nic.* viii. 11. 1161 b 8.

Against these shortcomings we must set some lessons of permanent value which the Greeks have taught us, and which have not lost their meaning for this age. We may still learn from Greek thinkers that the moral and intellectual well-being of the citizens ranks first among the ends of the State, and the wealth of nations second; that fame, empire, trade, material comforts all must be subordinated to this paramount end. A people as well as an individual ought to be possessed by the disinterested love of what is noble, *τὸ καλόν*: they ought to remember that there is an intrinsic excellence in one type of life as compared with another, and that the relative value of goods cannot be measured by their immediate social utility—a standard which is dependent on the guesswork of short-sighted politicians. Further, that while we should aim at nothing less comprehensive than the welfare of the whole people, we should not lower the level of our aim by looking only to the capacities of average humanity. The basis of civilisation must be laid broad: the mass of the people must receive the best culture of which they are capable. But there is a higher elevation of moral and intellectual achievement, of learning and science and spiritual culture, which is the crown of national existence, to which all nations that have been eminent in history have aspired, and which each in its degree has attained. This lofty and ideal perfection is not to be lost sight of even by the legislator, who in this age is being driven to concentrate all his efforts on raising the level of the lowest, on bettering their material condition, on mitigating the worst forms of misery and distress, and on removing the outward incentives to crime. It is one of the weakest points in most socialistic schemes that they narrow the horizon: they take a low standard of human well-being; and while they would make bad men better, and the squalid comfortable, and would bring hours of leisure into overworked and joyless lives, and would impart to every member of the community the rudiments of learning, yet they provide no satisfaction for the instinct of perfection: they rest content with the inferior standard, and do not care to develop the rich and many-sided manhood, which the Greeks prized, not excessively, but only too exclusively. To the Greeks as to Burke the State is "a partnership in all science, in all art, in every virtue, in all perfection." It is just this partnership in all perfection that practical politicians put out of sight. Not that science, art, literature, or philosophy can be created by the direct action of the Legislature. But it makes no little difference how the State, in its collective and corporate character, behaves towards each of these; in what honour or dishonour it holds them. The State may starve them with cold neglect, or it may admit its obligations towards them grudgingly and of necessity; or again it may act on the conviction that the higher culture, the quickened intellectual life of the community, is the concern of the whole nation.

By the Greeks, again, we are reminded that the State is an organic unity; that it is not the Government of the day and that it did not come into being with an electoral contest: that its action is the action of the community, and the laws which it makes are the expression of the people's will and claim the obedience of all. And as the State is not the same thing as a party or combination of parties, still less is it an aggregate of diverse and conflicting interests. In our own country in addition to the two great parties within the State, which are divided by momentous questions of public policy, there are at present various sections, cliques, and coteries, jostling and struggling together for representation in the supreme Parliament. They are technically known as "interests"—the landed interest, the manufacturing interest, the shipping interest, the labour interest, the liquor interest—these and many more besides; sectional interests one and all of them, which do not even rise to the dignity of party, because they are identified with no national policy or aims. Each is concerned with itself. The State is set aside. If Parliament should ever come to consist in the main of delegates representing these several interests, the wholeness, the soundness, the corporate unity of the State would be gravely imperilled.

And lastly the example and teaching of Greece recall to us that the State is not an abstraction, not a mechanism of government; it is the individuals who compose it; the State is the People. In ancient Athens it consisted of friends and neighbours, citizens who all sat together in the same assembly: with us it consists of vast groups of unknown fellow-countrymen, who yet have a common past and common hopes for the future. The City-state has grown into a nation, but it is as true now as in the days of Pericles that the greatness of a State lies not in the multitude of its inhabitants, not in its machinery, not in docks and arsenals, not even in its institutions; but in the great qualities of its individual citizens, in their capacity for high and unselfish effort and their devotion to the public good.

SOPHOCLES[1]

THE appearance of the first volume of a complete edition of Sophocles by Professor Jebb is an event of interest, not only to classical students, but to all who care for literature. No living English scholar unites in himself so many of the qualities which, for our generation, form the ideal of classical scholarship. He has the passion for beauty, the feeling for style and literary expression, the artistic enthusiasm of the Italian Renaissance. But he is moreover a laborious worker over a wide field; he has grasped the history of the ideas and usages of the ancient world, and presents his learning in forms of graceful and finished composition. While the distinctive move-

[1] This article was originally published as a notice of the first volume (*Oedipus Tyrannus*) of Professor Jebb's edition of Sophocles —a work which has now taken its rank among the great Editions of the Classics. Detailed criticism of detached passages is omitted in this reprint, and the latter portion of the paper has been enlarged.

ment of our own day in the province of classical criticism has been towards the union of the literary with the scientific spirit, the latter has tended to preponderate. The study of language and archaeology on the technical side seems at times to kill the literary sense. Professor Jebb has been largely affected by the scientific movement of the age; the growing influence upon him of the new critical and comparative methods may be traced in his successive writings. But the scientific influence has strengthened, not impaired, his literary perception by broadening the basis on which an appreciative judgment can be formed, and by adding clearness, completeness, and precision to his mode of statement and exposition.

After excursions into various domains of classical literature and archaeology, he has returned to Sophocles, the object of his earliest affections, with his brilliant powers enriched and invigorated by these wider studies. He is more erudite, more scientific, than before, but not less artistic.

This volume of Sophocles ought to appeal to the educated public through the fine literary criticism contained in the Introduction, and even more, perhaps, through the prose translation which accompanies the text. The translation, as Professor Jebb explains in his Preface, is intended primarily to be judged "from the stand-point of the commentator as an indispensable instrument of lucid interpretation." But he adds :—

> The second object which had been proposed to this edition regards educated readers generally, not classical students alone. It is my hope—whether a vain one or not I hardly know—that the English version facing the Greek text may induce some persons to read a play of Sophocles as they would read a great poem of a modern poet,—with no interposing nightmare of τύπτω as at Athens came between Thackeray and his instinctive sense of what was admirable in the nature and art around him,—but with free exercise of the mind and taste, thinking only of the drama itself, and of its qualities as such. Surely that is, above all things, what is to be desired by us just now in regard to all the worthiest literature of the world—that people should know some part of it *at first hand*, not merely through manuals of literary history or magazine articles.
>
> . . . Any one who had read thoroughly and intelligently a single play such as the *Oedipus Tyrannus* would have derived far more intellectual advantage from Greek literature, and would comprehend far better what it has signified in the spiritual history of mankind, than if he had committed to memory the names, dates, and abridged contents of a hundred Greek books ranging over half a dozen centuries.

It would be impossible to quote the innumerable felicities of the prose translation, or adequately to illustrate a quality which the Greeks call μετριότης—the reserve, the temperate strength, the harmonious perfection of the whole. A translator needs constantly to bear in mind the Greek proverb, "The half is greater than the whole"—a proverb whose truth has too often been forgotten by the authors of the Revised Version of the New Testament. Language must not be forced to go beyond its own capacities. No one else, it may be safely said, could have produced a translation in which the claims of the letter and the spirit are so finely reconciled.

The language of Sophocles may well strike despair into the translator or commentator. It is a mysterious union of popular[1] and literary idiom, of learning and originality. Apparently simple, it is full of subtle associations,[2] and charged with poetic memories of the past. Over and above its obvious sense it has a meaning and emotion which these memories and associations waken. It is a language of delicate suggestion and allusiveness, resembling in some measure the language of Virgil and of Milton. It means more—nay, at times something other—than it seems to say. Various lights and colours play about the words,[3] which

[1] For colloquial phrases see *O. T.* 336, 363, 971, 1008.

[2] *E.g.*, *O. T.* 161, Ἄρτεμιν, ἃ κυκλόεντ' ἀγορᾶς θρόνον εὐκλέα θάσσει 930, παντελὴς δάμαρ. See the notes on both passages.

[3] *E.g.* ὀφθαλμός *O. T.* 987.

defy strict analysis; when we attempt to reduce them to prosaic simplicity they elude our grasp. Without doing violence to Attic idiom, Sophocles freely handles familiar phrases, and puts a gentle pressure upon common words to extract from them a fresh significance.[1]

It sometimes becomes a nice question whether a word can, in some one or two passages, bear a meaning quite different from its current acceptation. It is doubtless the privilege of a poet to force a word back along the line of its own development in the direction of its etymology or of primitive usage. One of the boldest experiments of this kind is to be found in Tennyson's poem, "Love and Duty," where these lines occur:—

> Live—yet live—
> Shall sharpest pathos blight us, knowing all
> Life needs for life is possible to will—
> Live happy.

"Pathos" is here used in its old Greek sense of "suffering." The general tenor and context of the poem, as well as special phrases, such as "apathetic end," that precede, prepare us for this meaning. It remains, however, an open question

[1] See notes on *O. T.* 34, *δαιμόνων συναλλαγαῖς*; 420 and 1208, *λιμήν*; 728, *ὑποστραφείς*; 677, *ἴσος*.

whether the experiment is not too venturous. Now, some distinguished Greek scholars have supposed that in *Oed. Tyr.* 44-45 :—

> ὡς τοῖσιν ἐμπείροισι καὶ τὰς ξυμφορὰς
> ζώσας ὁρῶ μάλιστα τῶν βουλευμάτων,

the word *ξυμφοράς*, in combination with *τῶν βουλευμάτων*, has, contrary to its recognised usage, the meaning of *comparisons* (of counsels), on the analogy of the corresponding verb *ξυμφέρειν*. Professor Jebb rightly, as I think, decides against this view, and supports his opinion with equal learning and humour. But, it might be asked, is such a departure from usage more violent than Tennyson's "pathos"? Yes, and for this reason,—that in Tennyson the context is itself a sufficient guide, and places the meaning beyond all doubt, while in Sophocles the unfamiliar sense is at the best highly ambiguous, and comes on us with a shock of hardly pleasurable surprise.

Plutarch[1] records a striking statement made by Sophocles about himself, to the effect that, after he had outgrown the pompous style of Aeschylus (*τὸν Αἰσχύλου διαπεπαιχὼς ὄγκον*), he adopted a harsh and artificial manner (*τὸ πικρὸν*

[1] Plut. *De Profect. in Virt.* ch. vii.

καὶ κατάτεχνον), which he finally exchanged for that style which "is best suited for ethical portraiture." Now, his dramatic activity extended over sixty-two years, during which time he wrote one hundred and thirteen plays. His seven extant tragedies belong, it would seem, to the third of the periods above indicated and represent his mature style, which is equally removed from turgid grandeur and affected ingenuity; it expresses with unrivalled truth and delicacy the play of the idealised human emotions.

It requires a highly trained capacity to detect the niceties of the Sophoclean language, to note the deflections from ordinary usage, and to interpret the pregnant expressions of the poet without petrifying them into rigid forms which cannot contain them. Professor Jebb is gifted with a sympathetic insight into Greek idiom and the latent powers of the language. He has a remarkable—one might say a unique—faculty of infusing poetry into grammar, of leading his readers through particles, moods, and tenses, vividly to realise the dramatic situation and enter into the feelings of the speaker. Under his guidance we seem not so much to be engaged in a work of logical analysis or skilful dissection as to be following a vital process of growth and construction. We are admitted to watch the inner movements of the poet's thought and to see the motives which, in all probability, determined the choice of this or that word or phrase. The style of the tragic dialogue in particular has never been so justly appreciated or luminously interpreted as in this edition. Between the language of the dialogue and of the lyrical portions of a Greek play there is an important distinction to be borne in mind. In writing choral songs the dramatists had well-known models to follow, and employed a style that was prescribed by literary tradition. A new problem had to be solved when they came to the dialogue. Here they were entering upon new paths, and had difficulties to overcome not unlike those which were encountered by the first Greek historians and orators, in whose hands an artistic prose was shaped.

The dramatic poet, whose province it was to compress into a brief compass the portrayal of character in action, to depict the conflict between individual wills, to delineate the successive moments in the fortunes of the actors and the corresponding feelings awakened in their minds, needed a vehicle of literary expression which should convey reasonings terser and more compact, thought and emotion more concentrated, than could be conveyed through the epic or the lyrical style. Tragedy, moreover, even before it became in the hands of Euripides a poetical image of public debate in the law-courts and assemblies, could not but catch the tone and accent of civic life. Professor Jebb tells us in his Preface, that in the course of preparing his commentaries on the *Electra* and the *Ajax*, he "had been led to see more clearly the intimate relation which in certain respects exists between Greek tragic dialogue and Greek rhetorical prose, and to feel the desire of studying more closely the whole process by which Greek oratory had been developed." Thus it was "as a preparation in one department for the task of editing Sophocles that the special studies embodied in the *Attic Orators* had originally been undertaken."

These and kindred studies have supplied him with a wealth of material hitherto unused in interpreting the tragic dialogue, while his powers of lucid expression enable us to follow with ease the reconstructive effort of the commentator, and with him to trace the process by which the colloquial idiom is moulded anew as it passes through the imagination of the poet. None but a scholar who is imbued with Greek modes of thinking and feeling, and penetrated by the Greek spirit, could attempt such a task without falling into fanciful speculations. But not the least of Professor Jebb's virtues as a commentator is his perfect sanity and sobriety of judgment.

In discovering double meanings and constructions in the Sophoclean language much tact and caution are necessary. Conington, in his commentary on Virgil, had got hold of a true idea —one which may be applied to Sophocles as well as to Virgil—in seeking to disentangle the various associations and reminiscences which are woven into the texture of the Virgilian phrases, and to show the blended colours which meet in a single word. But even he is sometimes led to press the principle to a point at which the different meanings are not different only but mutually inconsistent. Take, for instance, his comment on *Aeneid* i. 748-9 :—

> Nec non et vario noctem sermone trahebat
> Infelix Dido.

Here he attempts to find in the phrase, *trahere noctem*, the double sense of "to speed the night along," and "to protract the night." "Perhaps," he says, "Virgil intended to blend the two notions in spite of their apparent inconsistency." The inconsistency, surely, is real as well as apparent.

Now the extension of a similar principle to Greek syntax requires to be very carefully guarded and explained, if we would avoid a confusion which in this case is so far worse than in the first, as it affects not a particular phrase only, but the whole thought of a sentence. No one, indeed, will deny that the Greek language admits of what the grammarians call "mixed" constructions, in which two modes of expressing the same thought have, as it were, met and contended, and neither has completely prevailed over the other. But commentators are too ready to shirk rather than to solve a grammatical difficulty by referring in vague terms to this principle; nay, there are notes in which moods and cases are subjected to a double grammatical government in such a way as to imply that contradictory ideas were together present in the mind of the writer. It seems to be assumed that a "mixed construction" naturally produces a confused thought. But the assumption is by no means true. A thought may be conveyed through forms which from the grammatical point of view are imperfectly fused, and yet the thought itself, which results from this imperfect fusion, need not be blurred or indistinct, much less self-contradictory. A clear thought often struggles for utterance, and fails to express itself in strict and logical form, not because the speaker does not know what he means, but because he is over-eager to say it.

That Greek modes of speech are too subtle and flexible to be bound by the rules of grammarians, that they break loose from such rigorous prescriptions and follow the ways of the living voice and the spontaneous movements of thought, is a fact which the commentator has often forgotten, and of which he needs again and again to be reminded. But some who have done good service in stating and illustrating this principle, have occasionally presented it in such a light as to suggest that in the days of Thucydides and Sophocles language was in so fluid a state and grammar so unfixed, that words might mean almost anything, and that clear thinking is as little to be looked for from the Periclean age as accurate writing. That Thucydides was writing in an ante-grammatical age is true only in the sense that he was writing in an age previous to grammarians. But there was grammar before there were grammarians, and a grammar, moreover, far more precise than was observed by the Elizabethan dramatists, who cannot be accepted as affording a perfect parallel to the Greek tragedians. The grammar of Sophocles is not, indeed, as strict and systematic as that of the Homeric poems; still it is part of a developed Attic idiom, whose normal usages had been firmly traced, in which moods, voices, tenses are in no way interchangeable, whose very irregularities were due rather to the desire for clearness and naturalness, than to confused modes of thought.

In Thucydides, and even in Sophocles, there are many experiments in words and in construction, many tentative and some hazardous forms of expression, which Aristophanes or Demosthenes would have rejected, but nothing which would warrant us in placing either author above the genius and idiom of the language. At what point neglect of grammar becomes violation of idiom cannot be stated in general terms. Special instances must be taken and scrutinised each on its own merits, and it is one of the marked features of Professor Jebb's edition that, in estimating the value of various readings or in justifying a phrase or construction, he faces the problem in each case, and lets us see how "irregular" grammar may yet be perfectly idiomatic. The elasticity of the Greek language is not license or caprice. It arises from the desire to add life and variety, to adjust new ideas to existing but inadequate forms of speech, to arrange the thought in a framework supplied by nature rather than by the laws of grammatical sequence and symmetry, so that the general form in which a sentence is cast influences the syntactical structure of the parts. Attraction, false analogy, sudden changes of construction—these and many other things are admitted by the Greeks to a degree that is unknown in Latin writers. The difficulty of the commentator lies not so much in stating the principle truly as in applying it correctly; and it is mainly by the application that the merits of grammatical criticism must be tested. I have heard the late Mr. R. Shilleto, towards the end of his life, say that the longer he lived the more reluctant he was to declare anything impossible in Greek. Such a saying would satisfy the most advanced believers in grammatical laxity. But when he came to grapple with the difficulties of the text, and to discuss whether some given expression was admissible in Greek, no one could more triumphantly vindicate the genius and the true idiom of the language.

One of the first questions that meets a commentator is, how far is it his duty to give alternative explanations. The natural bent of those whom we may call *οἱ ῥέοντες*—those who treat the Attic Greek of the middle of the fifth century B.C. as in a perfectly fluid and unstable condition—is to multiply such alternatives without giving any, or, at least, a sufficient reason for preferring one alternative to another. There are, doubtless, not a few passages where it would require a very audacious person to pronounce confidently between rival interpretations. Most scholars can recall lines over which they have hesitated long, when the balance seems so nicely poised that it depends on some accident of the moment—a passing mood or touch from without—to determine which way it shall decline. But this is true of poetic diction, not in Greek only, but in all languages, including our own. If, however, in every third or fourth line of a poem we are reduced to such honest doubts and waverings, we must infer either that the author writes badly, or that we have a very imperfect acquaintance with the language. It is to be hoped that our knowledge of Greek and Latin is not really so much a matter of guess-work as the numerous alternatives offered to us by classical editors would imply. Sometimes it may happen that we have in our own mind a strong conviction in favour of one definite interpretation, but that the impression is incommunicable; it rests on a sense or instinct which cannot be justified by argument. In such cases the final verdict must be left to the few who are acknowledged to possess the surest insight and the finest tact in handling language. There is no other court of appeal.

But putting aside such cases, there are, as a rule, valid grounds on which a decision may be based. It is almost as serious an error for a commentator to place side by side several interpretations without furnishing the materials for arriving at a rational conclusion, as it would be for a writer on etymology to give us an open choice between a guess of Plato's and a scientific result of comparative philology. Many current interpretations are demonstrably wrong, and the only sufficient excuse for mentioning them at all is that they are still current, and therefore need refutation. But the mere fact that some great name is associated with an absurd interpretation is hardly a plea for reviving it, unless it happens to raise a point of interest in the history of literary criticism. Still less ought the stray fancies of obscurer critics to be recorded in the notes among a series of other options equally ingenious, but no less certainly wrong. In nine cases out of ten the author doubtless had a single meaning, and it is the business of one who interprets him to tell us what he conceives that meaning to have been, and to show the grounds of his decision. The practice observed by Professor Jebb in this edition has, on the whole, been to mention various interpretations only where there is room for serious and legitimate doubt as to the meaning of the poet. He ignores such alternatives as are not commended either by their intrinsic merit or by a weight of authority which cannot be disregarded. Yet his notes, while generally avoiding direct refutation, incidentally sweep aside a large mass of rubbish which had found its way into many editions.

This is not the place to discuss in detail the subject of conjectural emendations. No one, however, who has studied the history of textual criticism, will be inclined to slight the gains that scholarship has won through the labours in this department, not only of past generations of scholars, but in our own day of such men as Cobet (in spite of rashness) and Madvig. Those who judge Madvig only by his *Adversaria Critica*, where admirable theory is united to some very dubious practice, and who think of him as the author of a few brilliant and of many superfluous emendations of Greek prose, not to mention certain tasteless and even unmetrical verse emendations, ought to study him at his best in the *De Finibus* of Cicero and in his emendations of Livy, whose pages have been illuminated under his touch. In passing, it may be observed that Latin prose authors, from one point of view, afford the best field for the exercise of an emendator's faculty, owing to the very rigour and precision of Latin prose idiom. But, after all, the limits within which such a second-sight as Bentley claimed for himself—"a certain divining tact and inspiration"—can profitably be employed, are singularly narrow. Many sanguine hopes would be abated if we did but reflect what a small percentage of conjectures have borne the test of time and received the stamp of scientific certitude.

Of all authors Sophocles is one of the most perilous for a critic to tamper with:—

His style (says Professor Jebb, p. lviii) is not seldom analogous to that of Virgil in this respect, that, when his instinct felt a phrase to be truly and finely expressive he left the logical analysis of it to the discretion of grammarians then unborn. I might instance νῦν πᾶσι χαίρω (*O. T.* 596). Such a skill may easily provoke the heavy hand of prosaic correction; and, if it requires sympathy to interpret and defend it, it also requires, when it has once been marred, a very tender and very temperate touch in any attempt to restore it.

Nothing could be better said; and the caution was never more needed than to-day, when Greek texts are being not emended but re-written. Scholarship at this moment has as much to fear from erudite absurdities as from almost any other cause. The worst of it is that the figments of emendators claim admission in the name of common sense, which frequently serves only as a mask for ignorance of Greek idiom. Ingenuity without insight, encyclopaedic study without judgment or perception, these are the things that corrupt the classics and bring learning itself into disrepute. Professor Jebb has been faithful to the canons he himself has laid down about emendation. He deals in conjecture only where the reading of the MSS. is confessedly hopeless. His own emendations in the *Oedipus Tyrannus* are fourteen in number, of which he admits nine into the text. Most of these are highly plausible and two of them attain as nearly as can be to certainty.[1]

It is not possible here to convey any idea of the interest of the commentary itself—of the sagacity and discrimination with which the exact force of words and phrases[2] and the connexion of thought are seized and elucidated. Those who study the book will find it to be, in the best sense of the word, original,—not by startling conjecture and paradox, but in power of delicate insight and interpretation, in a masterly handling of difficulties, and in the apprehension of each part and every detail in its bearing on the whole.

When we pass from verbal criticism to the substance of this play, we find ourselves confronted with a great moral question—How are suffering

[1] The first and most striking occurs in line 1218, where the MSS. have *δύρομαι γὰρ ὡς περίαλλα ἰαχέων* (*vv. ll.* *περίαλα*, *ἀχέων*) *ἐκ στομάτων*. Professor Jebb's brilliant restoration is *δύρομαι γὰρ ὥσπερ ἰάλεμον χέων ἐκ στομάτων*, "I wail as one who pours a dirge from his lips." The second of such corrections is in 1280, where the simple change of *κακά* to *κατά* make perfect sense of the passage.

[2] See, for instance, the notes on 35 (*ἐξέλυσας δασμόν*), 227 (*ὑπεξελεῖν*), 313 (*ῥῦσαι μίασμα*), 354 (*ἐξεκίνησας ῥῆμα*), 628 (*ἀρκτέον*), 674 (*θυμοῦ περάσῃς*), 709 (*μαντικῆς ἔχον τέχνης*), 790 (*προὐφάνη λέγων*), 846 (*οἰόζωνος*), 978 (*πρόνοια*), 997 (*ἡ Κόρινθος . . . ἀπῳκεῖτο*), 1077 (*βουλήσομαι*), 1483 (*προὐξένησαν*). The delicate use of the particles is vividly interpreted in the notes to this edition (*e.g.* 105, 342, 822, 852, 1030).

and guilt related according to the view of Sophocles? We have in this play an eminent example of a man, not indeed perfect, yet noble and of good intentions, who is led on by a train of events that baffled human foresight into unconscious crimes and overwhelming calamity. Is it that the gods take a wanton pleasure in smiting down, age after age, a mighty house like that of the Labdacidae? Or is there between the deeds and fortunes of Oedipus an inward and moral connexion such that his sufferings are a punishment for defects of character, great as the disproportion may seem to be between the penalty and the fault? Or, again, is there some other explanation, consonant with Greek feeling and with what we know of the religious temper of Sophocles?

There was, no doubt, a popular idea that the gods were jealous of man, in whom they saw a restless and dangerous rival. They watched his progress, they resented his achievements, and delighted to overthrow him unawares. Not the impious spirits only who grasped at divine privileges incurred their hostility. They were envious even of the perfect happiness of man and wife. Penelope, when she has made proof of Odysseus and knows him again for her lord, exclaims, "It is the gods that gave us trouble, the gods who were jealous that we should abide together and have joy of our youth and come to the threshold of old age."[1] The benefactors of mankind are also among their victims; for in the triumphs of civilising genius they saw an encroachment upon their own rights. Kings and potentates at the height of their greatness stood most in peril of attack from these jealous powers, and at such moments it was their wisdom to appease the gods with the best thing they had. Man was permitted to enjoy a certain limited measure of prosperity; but he must learn to know his place. The distinction must not be effaced between the divine and the human nature.

In the Homeric poems there are as yet but few traces of the divine Jealousy. The idea gathered strength during the period of the Tyrannies; mainly, as it would seem, owing to the impressive catastrophes, the warning examples, of that age. Herodotus, more than any other Greek author, reflects the features of the primitive belief. One view under which he exhibits the gods is that of privileged despots who resent all eminence in others, and who take a malignant delight in level-

[1] *Odyss.* xxiii. 210-12.

ling down human greatness to a safe mediocrity.[1] It is the view expressed by Aesop, who, when asked what was Zeus engaged in, answered, "In humbling the exalted and in exalting the humble."[2] Yet a righteous purpose is not unseldom seen to govern the divine dealings. The guilty are punished even if the innocent share their doom; the working of moral motives modifies the capricious action of the Olympian powers. Between these two aspects of the government of the world Herodotus wavers. On the whole he is able to discern a righteous plan in the ordering of events. But the popular creed held its ground long and tenaciously. How persistent it was may be inferred from the protests of Plato,[3] of Aristotle,[4]—who seldom meddles with such subjects,—and of Plutarch.[5] The daemonic force which appeared to be at work in shaping human destiny, and which was personified as divine Jealousy (*Φθόνος*), always remains below the surface of Greek history; this power

[1] Herod. i. 32; iii. 40; vii. 10; vii. 46. Cp. Thucyd. vii. 77. 4.

[2] Diog. Laert. i. 3, τὰ μὲν ὑψηλὰ ταπεινῶν, τὰ δὲ ταπεινὰ ὑψῶν.

[3] *Phaedr.* 247 A, φθόνος γὰρ ἔξω θείου χόρου ἵσταται.

[4] *Met.* i. 2. 983 a 2, ἀλλ' οὔτε τὸ θεῖον φθονερὸν ἐνδέχεται εἶναι, ἀλλὰ καὶ κατὰ τὴν παροιμίαν πολλὰ ψεύδονται ἀοιδοί, οὔτε κ.τ.λ.

[5] *Non posse suaviter, etc.*, ch. 22, ἀγαθὸς γάρ ἐστιν (sc. ὁ θεός), ἀγαθῷ δὲ περὶ οὐδενὸς ἐγγίγνεται φθόνος.

came to be recognised as an independent deity, and received embodiment in art. Even Pindar, who cast off so many of the grosser elements of the received religion, is not able to rid himself of this belief. In celebrating his victorious athletes he is apprehensive lest such high praise may bring down the envy of the immortals. Visions rise before him of the great ones of the earth who had mounted too high and were suddenly struck low. He checks himself in his course ; he utters a counsel of humility or a pious prayer that envy may be averted.

It was an incomparable service that Aeschylus rendered in attempting to correct and enlighten this primitive belief. He shared the sentiment which saw in every great reverse of fortune a judicial act ; but the sentence, as he read it, was not pronounced by jealous or capricious powers, but by a supreme and moral governor of the universe. In the course of events and in all human destinies he traced the righteous and overruling hand of Zeus, "the Almighty," "King of Kings," "who rewards all men according to their works." Everywhere and in all cases there is an inner and necessary connexion between men's actions and their outward fortunes. Not only in the vicissitudes of nations and families, but also in the history of individuals, the same law of moral retribution holds good. Each man fares according to his deserving; even the individual life, viewed in its happiness and misery, is long enough to justify the ways of God to man. In Aeschylus Nemesis or divine Justice displaces the divine Jealousy. The notion of rightness or justness is never absent from the word. In the drama of India the wrath of the gods is called down by the trifling omission of a religious formula. In the Greek drama Nemesis is the penalty of wrongdoing. It punishes, above all, that Insolence or *ὕβρις* which has its root in want of reverence and want of self-knowledge, which is the expression of a self-centred will recognising no power outside itself, and knowing no law but its own impulses. Nemesis is not a caprice.

This Insolence in the Greek tragedy is the deepest source of moral evil. It is the spirit of blind self-reliance which does not respect eternal ordinances, which seeks to overpass the bounds set for mortality and ignores the conditions of existence. It is opposed to both *αἰδώς* and *σωφροσύνη*. In the sphere of religion it is manifested not only in the irreverent deed, but in the presumptuous word or thought—in a pride that is untempered by the sense of human frailty. In the sphere of human relations it shows itself in the arrogance of the oriental monarch, in the shout of triumph over the fallen foe, in the contempt of the suppliant, in the disregard of others' rights and feelings. The Nemesis that overtakes it is the retribution that follows upon sin. Nothing can be more false than to confound the Nemesis of Greek tragedy with the Jealousy of the gods as popularly conceived, or to find the distinctive difference between the classical and the modern drama in the transition from the sway of jealous gods to the idea of moral retribution. The tragic Nemesis of the Greeks rests not on a mere feeling of artistic measure or proportion, but on the conviction of an eternal law of conduct whose violation brings punishment. The motto of the Aeschylean drama is, "The guilty suffers" (δράσαντι παθεῖν); crime it is that brings disaster and final ruin.

If some tragedies of Aeschylus seem at first sight to rest under a sombre fatalism or to be presided over by the vigilance of jealous gods, a closer study will show that here too events are not guided by blind or arbitrary forces, but are the outcome of character and subject to moral laws.

In the *Agamemnon*, for example, the shadow of doom throws itself forward from the first; the atmosphere is charged with sinister presentiments, even in the midst of victory. The keynote of suspicion and mystery is struck by the watchman. Each successive song of the Chorus either calls up some old and dark reminiscence, or hints at some new foreboding. Throughout, there runs the sense of crime committed that must needs be expiated. The Chorus—here clearly the mouthpiece of the poet—expressly dissents from the old belief that mere prosperity produces calamity (v. 750). The guilt that Agamemnon had incurred in slaying Iphigeneia, is visited on him now in the hour of his triumph when he is flushed with pride and insolence. At such a time Nemesis is most to be dreaded, not because the gods are jealous, but because men are then apt to become reckless.

Other popular beliefs were in like manner newly interpreted by Aeschylus. The curse of a father was thought to have an almost magical efficacy and to carry with it a certainty of fulfilment. Originally, perhaps, it was associated with the exercise of certain judicial powers by the parent. In any case it is as old as Homer.[1] It is the

[1] *Iliad* ix. 453, 566; *Odyss.* ii. 135.

Greek parallel to the patriarchal blessing of the Hebrews. The latter idea was unfamiliar to Greek thought, though Plato[1] tentatively suggests that, if the imprecation of a father is divinely ratified, his prayers for blessing may well have in them a similar virtue. The operation of the curse, as exhibited both in Aeschylus and in Sophocles, is part of a moral law. It is no arbitrary sentence of doom. Once it has gone forth it is irrevocable, but it is not pronounced except over those who are already hardened offenders. On them it invokes not suffering merely but fresh guilt. It is, as it were, a solemn excommunication. Morally, it is based on the conviction that there are some sins, such as filial impiety, which leave no place for repentance. The imprecation uttered by Oedipus upon his sons in the *Oedipus Coloneus* is so terrible that modern imitators of Sophocles prefer to make Oedipus relent. But the Greek Oedipus is implacable. He speaks not merely as the aggrieved father, but as the representative of outraged justice, the spokesman of the Erinys; unlike Lear, whose imprecation on Goneril, in its refinement of cruelty, betrays a mind maddened by the sense

[1] *Laws* xi. 931 C.

of a personal wrong. The victims of the curse in Aeschylus employ the language of fatalism. They throw themselves with a recklessness half of triumph, half of despair, into fulfilling the prophecy of evil. The curse has gone forth; let it work; they will swim with wind and stream:

> ἐπεὶ τὸ πρᾶγμα κάρτ᾽ ἐπισπέρχει θεός,
> ἴτω κατ᾽ οὖρον κῦμα Κωκυτοῦ λαχὸν
> Φοίβῳ στυγηθὲν πᾶν τὸ Λαΐου γένος.[1]

Such is the tone of Eteocles in the *Thebans*. Yet it is plain that though Eteocles speaks as a fatalist, he acts as a free man.

The problem of fate and free-will presented itself again, and in a more complex form, in the received doctrine of an hereditary curse. Legend told of families in which, owing to some ancestral crime, the taint of guilt was transmitted in the blood, and generation after generation was visited by the anger of the gods. "If the criminals escape," writes Solon,[2] "and the doom of the gods overtakes them not yet—soon or late the doom comes: the guiltless children or descendants pay the forfeit." The idea had its origin in primitive

[1] *Theb.* 689-91.
[2] Solon xiii. 29-32 (Bergk).

times when the solidarity of the family was strongly felt. The individual as a moral being was hardly kept distinct from the community to which he belonged. If one member of the community committed a crime all his family paid the penalty, either as fellow-sufferers with him or as suffering vicariously on his behalf. The guilt as well as the punishment was supposed to be corporate. Hence arose the idea of a curse bequeathed through successive generations, entailing on posterity not suffering merely but sin. The hold that this doctrine had over the popular consciousness, and its influence on practical politics, is attested by repeated incidents in the history of the Alcmaeonidae, who in the person of Megacles had incurred the pollution of a sacrilegious murder.

The question of corporate guilt and of long-delayed punishment was one which troubled the conscience of Greece down to a late period of her history. Euripides, so Plutarch says,[1] boldly accused the gods of injustice in visiting the sins of the parents upon the children (*τὰ τῶν τεκόντων σφάλματα εἰς τοὺς ἐγγόνους τρέποντας*). It was

[1] Plut. *De Ser. Num. Vind.* ch. 12; cp. Eur. *Hippol.* 831-33, 1378-83, Fr. 83 (Nauck).

in his manner to make a seasoned protest against the moral inconsistencies which he discovered in the popular theology. In the argument addressed by Tyndareus to Menelaus[1] he denounces the primitive law of vengeance, which gave religious sanction to the deed of Orestes. Blood calls for blood; each crime becomes a new link in a series of guilty acts; where can an end be found? In a similar spirit he appears to have dealt with the kindred doctrine here under consideration. Prose writers, too, other than the philosophers, show their dissatisfaction with this tenet of the popular theology. Isocrates[2] praises the superior piety of the Egyptians, who held that the penalty of each misdeed is exacted at the moment, and not put off to a later generation. In Plutarch's tract *De Sera Numinis Vindicta* the same problem is discussed on various sides. Some of the difficulties are met that are inherent in the proverb, "The mills of the gods grind slow, but they grind small" (ὀψὲ θεῶν ἀλέουσι μύλοι, ἀλέουσι δὲ λεπτά). Plutarch himself piously supports the prevalent belief in the curse in a house. Sometimes, he argues (ch. xv.-xvi. cp. ch. xxi.), it is a city, sometimes a race, on which the wrath of the god

[1] Eur. *Orest.* 491-525. [2] Isocr. *Busiris*, xi. 25.

descends.[1] In either case the principle of justice is the same. A city is a kind of living organism, it has a continuous existence, a unity, a personality not unlike that of the individual. It is morally responsible for its past. A race, too, has a like continuity of its own; it preserves certain dominant characteristics, birthmarks of the family, which, if vicious, need a corrective discipline as often as they reappear in successive generations. The analogy, however imperfect, is interesting and worth noting, though it does not go far to vindicate the view that is upheld.

The personal conviction of Aeschylus as to this problem is to be gathered from the dramatic presentation of the facts, not from the arguments of rival disputants. In one vital particular he modifies the popular belief. Not actual guilt, but the tendency to guilt is inherited. A man is master of his own fate; he may foster the tendency, or he may resist it. An act of will is necessary to wake the curse into life. The chain of crime may at any point be

[1] Similarly Pausanias gives examples of punishment of civic guilt being postponed for several generations; *e.g.* i. 36. 3; iv. 17. 3; vii. 15. 3. See an interesting article on "Hebrew and Greek Ideas of Providence and Retribution," by C. G. Montefiore in the *Jewish Quarterly Review* for July 1893.

broken, though the poet rather exhibits, for the most part, the natural continuity of guilt; that as crime engenders crime in the individual heart, so in a house the guilt of the fathers tends to lead the children into new guilt and to extend itself over a whole race. There is a striking resemblance between the language in which Aeschylus and George Eliot describe the self-productive energy of evil. In the words of Aeschylus[1]: "The impious deed leaves after it a larger progeny, all in the likeness of the parent stock." In the more elaborated phrase of George Eliot: "Our deeds are like children that are born to us; they live and act apart from our will: nay, children may be strangled, but deeds never; they have an indestructible life both in and out of our consciousness."

Still Aeschylus never allows human freedom to be obliterated, even in the members of a tainted race. By an initial act of man's free-will the latent guilt is evoked. In this he departs from the popular theology and saves morality. He handles those myths which deal with the domestic curse in much the same spirit as he treats the doctrine of divine Infatuation. The popular form of that doctrine is expressed, for instance, by

[1] *Agam.* 758-60.

Theognis,[1]—that a man of good intentions is often misled by some supernatural power into grievous transgressions, so that evil appears to him good and good evil. Aeschylus, too, recognises in certain forms of mental blindness a divine influence. There is a malady of the mind (*νόσος φρενῶν*) a heaven-sent hurt (*θεοβλάβεια*), which drives the sinner to destruction. This infatuation or Ate is a clouding both of heart and of intellect; it is also both the penalty and the parent of crime. But only when a man has wilfully set his face towards evil, when, like Xerxes in the *Persae*, or Ajax in the play of Sophocles, he has striven to rise above human limits, or like Creon in the *Antigone* has been guilty of obdurate impiety, is a moral darkening inflicted on him in judicial anger. Here Aeschylus and Sophocles agree. As we read in the Old Testament that "the Lord hardened Pharaoh's heart," so in Aeschylus, "when a man is hasting to his ruin the god helps him on."[2] It is the dark converse of "God helps those who help themselves." "With wisdom," says Sophocles,

[1] Theogn. 402-406.

[2] *Pers.* 742, *ἀλλ' ὅταν σπεύδῃ τις αὐτός, χὠ θεὸς συνάπτεται.* Cp. Aesch. Fr. 386 (Nauck) *φιλεῖ δὲ τῷ κάμνοντι συσπεύδειν θεός*: and 294, *ἀπάτης δικαίας οὐκ ἀποστατεῖ θεός.* See also Lycurg. *In Leocr.* § 91, 92.

"hath some one given forth the famous saying, that evil seems good soon or late to him whose mind the god draws to mischief."[1]

The doctrine of an inherited tendency towards guilt in a house reminds us, on one side, of the doctrine of original sin as the consequence of Adam's sin; and, on another, of modern theories of inherited qualities. If neither of these can be called fatalism, equally inapplicable is the word to the teaching of the Greek poets.

Much misconception has prevailed as to the place of Fate in the Greek drama. We are apt to confuse the meaning of the Greek word Moira, of which "Destiny" is in general the nearest equivalent, by associations derived from later controversies about free-will. Viewed etymologically its primary idea is that of *distribution*; and its usage suggests not so much that which is predestined, as that which is appointed as part of the moral order of the universe; and in this sense we find the corresponding adjective *μόρσιμος* applied even to the marriage tie as ordained between man and wife.[2] There is nothing in the normal use of the word to give prominence to the thought that the details of the individual life are mapped out

[1] *Antig.* 621-24 (Jebb's trans.). [2] Aesch. *Eum.* 217.

according to a predetermined plan and sequence. Already in Homer it has a twofold usage. On the one hand it is *what is decreed*—a poetic expression for that fundamental order of things which later prose writers would call φύσις. On the other hand, it is the power that regulates the course of human affairs, allotting to all their proper place. This power is supreme over gods as well as men, though in more than one instance Zeus thinks of attempting to defeat it in the interests of some favourite. But as the stream of Greek thought ran clearer such discord between the ruling powers of the universe became an offence. In the *Prometheus*, indeed, of Aeschylus there is still a conflict between Zeus and Necessity—Necessity as guided by "the triple Moirai and the mindful Erinyes"[1]—and so long as it lasts Zeus cannot be at one with Justice. But the Zeus of the *Prometheus* is not the great Omnipotent, the highest impersonation of godhead. At the time at which the dramatic action is laid he is still the god of a passing epoch, when the turmoil of contending dynasties was hardly subdued, and might was the only right. His will comes into collision with an inscrutable power against which he cannot

[1] *Prom.* 516.

prevail. Elsewhere in Aeschylus the course of events is under the ordered and developed rule of Zeus. The decrees of Destiny are in Aeschylus, as they already were in Pindar,[1] identified with his will. A perfect harmony has been established. "That which is destined will surely be accomplished; the great purposes of Zeus may not be transgressed."[2] But the more abstract conception of Moira was not superseded: it was the sum of those mysterious forces which limit human life and act on it from outside. In obedience to a Greek instinct the poets generally attribute to the Olympian gods the happy events of life, while they ascribe misfortune to the more impersonal and darker power, Moira.

In all this, however, the will of man is not, as we are sometimes told, paralysed by Destiny, by an overhanging doom which "does not leave him even an illusion of liberty" (Mazzini). Man combats his destiny; if he falls, he does so after exhibiting an almost Titanic energy of will. How different this is from the dramas of genuine fatalism!

[1] Pind. *Nem.* iv. 61, *τὸ μόρσιμον Διόθεν πεπρωμένον ἔκφερεν.*

[2] Aesch. *Suppl.* 1047; cp. *Eum.* 1045, Ζεὺς ὁ πανόπτας οὕτω Μοῖρά τε συγκατέβα. *Choeph.* 306, ἀλλ' ὦ μεγάλαι Μοῖραι, Διόθεν τῇδε τελευτᾶν. Pausanias mentions Μοιραγέτης as an epithet of Zeus (v. 15; viii. 37, etc.).

In the dramas of India the actors in no sense rely on their own efforts; their virtue is passive resignation and self-effacement: it is for the gods to cut the knots of the tragedy. In the Greek drama the power of an overruling Destiny is no more subversive of liberty in the case of men than the similar power in Homer is of the liberty of the gods. They are both free, men and gods, but free within certain limits. Outside this circle of freedom there are great unknown forces which hem in man's life and assail it. The more these powers of outward circumstance are magnified, the more impressive is the assertion of human free-will in the struggle against them. This is just what we find in Aeschylus. He is haunted by the feeling of the strange forces which play upon man from without; of the tendencies which perpetuate themselves in the blood and link together the generations as if they were a living whole. All the framework in which life was set belonged to a supernatural order, and such facts were together classed as Destiny. It is the element of mystery and the sense of the supernatural that has made Aeschylus sometimes appear more fatalistic than the other Greek poets. The religious view pervades his tragedies; he is a theologian as much as he is an artist. But his dramas so far from being fatalistic are in truth from end to end a vindication of human freedom.

Returning now to our main point we notice an important distinction between suffering for another and being punished for another. The first is a natural and physical process, a fact proved by experience. The second implies a judicial act—one which, when ascribed to the Deity, is an unauthorised inference from, or interpretation of, a fact. Punishment implies guilt, and the notion of an innocent man being punished for the guilty is a moral contradiction. The innocent man may and does suffer for the guilty; that he should be punished for the guilty is inconceivable, for guilt and with it moral condemnation are intransferable. To speak, therefore, of *Vicarious Suffering* has nothing in it to shock morality: *Vicarious Punishment* (if the full meaning of the idea is realised) is immoral. The tragedians show a consciousness of this distinction. The popular view was that guilt was inherited,—that is, that the children are punished for their fathers' sins. The view of Aeschylus —and of Sophocles also, so far as he touches the problem on this side—was that a tendency towards guilt is inherited, but this tendency does not annihilate man's free-will. If, therefore, the children are punished, they are punished for their own sins. But Sophocles saw the further truth, that innocent children may suffer for their fathers' sins.

The purification of this special doctrine of the popular religion, which was effected in Greece by the poets, was effected among the Jews by the prophets. The phrase, "visiting the sins of the fathers upon the children," was open to a double interpretation, — either that the children were punished judicially for their fathers' sins, or that the children suffered in the course of nature for their fathers' sins. The Jews for a long time interpreted the words of the second commandment in the first sense, just as the Greeks so interpreted the idea of a curse in the house. But Ezekiel (ch. xviii.), in clearer tones even than the Greek poets, rejected the first interpretation, and freed the notion of moral responsibility from all ties of blood relationship. "What mean ye, that ye use this proverb, The fathers have eaten sour grapes, and the children's teeth are set on edge? . . . The soul that sinneth it shall die. The son shall not bear the iniquity of the father, neither shall the father bear the iniquity of the son." The same truth had occurred early to the mind of India. In the *Ramayana* these striking words occur: "A father, a mother, a son, whether in this world or the next, eats only the fruit of his own works; a father is not recompensed or punished for his son, neither a son for his father. Each of these by his own actions gives birth to good or evil."

The doctrine, then, of the hereditary curse, as it is exhibited in the Greek poets, is not one of fatalism. Remembering the distinction between Vicarious Suffering, which is a natural process, and Vicarious Punishment, which is a penal sentence, we observe that the second of these ideas, which alone is fatalistic and immoral, is nowhere to be found,—not in Sophocles any more than in Aeschylus. It was part of the popular creed of Greece which was discarded by the tragedians.

So long as divine justice was believed to assert itself in the earthly life of the individual, it was natural that moral character should be judged by outward happiness, and that guilt and suffering should be inseparably associated. But there comes a time in the history of every people when the old theory of life, that the good always prosper and the bad are punished, has to yield before the stress of facts. Sophocles is the first of the Greeks who has clearly realised that suffering is not always penal, that it has other functions to discharge in the divine economy. The suffering of innocent children for the sins of the fathers, which Sophocles touches lightly, is comprised under the wider law of human suffering, in interpreting which he has made a great step in advance upon Aeschylus. He has penetrated into many aspects and meanings of suffering which were hitherto undiscerned. He stands midway between Aeschylus, who sees in it nothing but the working of retributive justice, and the sceptical theory of the succeeding age, that unmerited suffering is due to carelessness on the part of the gods. Having seized the central truth of the sufferings of the righteous — god - sent visitations, *θεῖαι τύχαι,* not the penalties of sin— he was able to accept many of the popular legends almost as they stood, and to breathe into them a moral meaning. It is not that there is in him, as some have thought, an incipient severance between morality and religion; that he has receded from the higher ground occupied by Aeschylus and lapsed into popular superstition. Aeschylus, for whom suffering was penal in intention, found in the legends a more intractable material; he was often obliged to remould and transform where Sophocles had merely to interpret anew. Of the primitive elements which Sophocles retains, those only can be held still to savour of popular superstition which are outside the action of the drama and among the supposed antecedents of the plot. These extraneous parts he is not always at pains to bring under the laws either of morality or of probability.

Undeserved suffering, while it is exhibited in Sophocles under various lights, always appears as part of the permitted evil which is a condition of a just and harmoniously ordered universe. It is foreseen in the counsels of the gods. It may,[1] as in the *Antigone*, serve to vindicate the higher laws by which the moral government of the world is maintained; or, as in the *Philoctetes* and *Trachiniae*, to advance a preordained and divine purpose; or, as in the *Philoctetes* and *Oedipus Coloneus*, to educate character. Sophocles deepens the meaning of the Greek proverb, "Man learns by suffering" (παθήματα μαθήματα). He raises it from a prudential or a moral maxim into a religious mystery. He anticipates the faith of

[1] See Mr. E. Abbott's "Essay on Sophocles" in *Hellenica* (Rivingtons, 1880), pp. 58, 59.

Plato,[1] that when a man is beloved of the gods, even poverty, sickness, and other sufferings can turn out only for his good. The *Oedipus Coloneus* affords the most perfect instance of the man whom adversity has sorely tried, and on whom it has had not indeed a softening, but a chastening and enlightening influence. Though this play was probably composed at a considerably later date than the *Oedipus Tyrannus*, and though each play is dramatically complete in itself, yet if we would learn the maturest thought of Sophocles upon the whole theme, we must study the *Oedipus Tyrannus* in the light of the sequel. Oedipus, it is true, is not a perfect character; he has flaws of temper and judgment; but not in these must we seek the explanation of his history. The poet indicates clearly that his calamities are to be traced to the inherent feebleness and short-sightedness of man, the obverse side of which is the divine foreknowledge; that his sufferings are in truth unmerited, and for that very reason have no power to subdue the soul. Oedipus has, of his own free-will, committed deeds which would be the most heinous of crimes had they been done with knowledge. Popular sentiment would have ascribed them

[1] *Rep.* x. 613 A.

to a divine Infatuation, which though inflicted arbitrarily and not as a judicial sentence, yet was supposed to leave the agent responsible for what he did.

Here, as in other plays, Sophocles fixes our attention on the difference between crime and involuntary error. The old belief of the Greeks, as of the Jews, was that an outward act could in itself constitute a crime; the guilt did not depend on the knowledge or intention of the agent. If pollution was incurred, some ritual expiation was necessary to wipe out the stain. Accidental homicide needed such a cleansing rite no less than voluntary murder. Even the lifeless instruments of a crime, stones or other weapons, had to pass through a purificatory process. Sophocles in the *Oedipus Coloneus* distinguishes between the inward and the outward quality of an act, between moral and ceremonial purity. In harmony with the religion of Apollo,[1] he discovers that the heart may be pure even where the hands have not been clean. As it is expressed in a fragment of his own: "The unwitting sin makes no man bad."[2] In the eye of religion Oedipus, in the *Oedipus*

[1] See p. 67.

[2] Soph. Fr. 599 (Nauck), ἄκων δ' ἁμαρτὼν οὔ τις ἀνθρώπων κακός.

Coloneus, is still a guilty man. The breach of the divine law leaves a stain, though the offender may have been the unconscious agent of a higher power. But whatever the ritual defilement, there is here moral innocence, and Oedipus himself asserts it. We hardly recognise him now as the man from whom we parted in the *Oedipus Tyrannus* in the first transport of horror and remorse. His old fiery temper is indeed still ready to blaze forth. But suffering has wrought on him far otherwise than on Lear, whose weak and passionate nature it unhinged, and with whom the thought that he himself was mainly to blame embittered his anger and turned grief into despair. Oedipus has disencumbered himself of a past which is not truly part of himself. In the school of suffering his inborn nobleness of character has come out. The long years have taught him resignation.[1] In spite of troubled memories he is at peace with himself and reconciled to heaven. He has read the facts of his past life in another light. He has pondered the ancient oracles of Apollo, which predicted to him at once his doom and his final rest. His inward eye has

[1] *O.C.* 7, *στέργειν γὰρ αἱ πάθαι με χὠ χρόνος ξυνὼν | μακρὸς διδάσκει.* Cp. Soph. Fr. 595 (Nauck), *πόλλ' ἐν κακοῖσι θυμὸς εὐνηθεὶς ὁρᾷ.*

been purged, and with newly won spiritual insight he thinks of himself as a man set apart by the gods for their own mysterious purposes. He bears himself with the calm and dignity of one who knows that he is obeying their express summons and has a high destiny to fulfil. The unconscious sin is expiated; and he who was the victim of divine anger, the accursed thing that polluted the city, is now the vehicle of blessing to the land that receives him. A sufferer not a sinner, restored to the favour of the gods, he finds in that favour and in the honours that await him, an ample recompense for all he has endured—

> Nothing is here for tears, nothing to wail,
> Or knock the breast; no weakness, no contempt,
> Dispraise or blame; nothing but well and fair,
> And what may quiet us in a death so noble.

Both Aeschylus and Sophocles attained to the conception of a righteous order of the world under the sovereign rule of Zeus. Sophocles had not, indeed, the speculative insight of Aeschylus, nor did he grapple so strenuously with the deepest problems of existence. Yet he did not yield the ground won by Aeschylus, or renounce the moral gains that had been bequeathed by him. In one religious idea, as we have seen—in his interpretation of human suffering—he even advanced beyond his predecessor. Aeschylus believed in an unseen and guiding Power, that dispenses rewards and punishments to individuals and communities, on principles of unerring justice. In Sophocles the divine righteousness asserts itself not in the award of happiness or misery to the individual, but in the providential wisdom which assigns to each individual his place and function in a universal moral order. Unmerited suffering here receives at least a partial explanation.

THE MELANCHOLY OF THE GREEKS

WE are commonly inclined to think of the Greeks as a people, and the only people, who for a brief space in the history of mankind looked on the universe with a clear and untroubled spirit; who in the freshness of their powers, and with a finely gifted nature, in which mind and body, heart and intellect, reason and imagination perfectly conspired together, seized life in its wholeness, and drew from it the full measure of rational delight which it is capable of affording. The world of the unseen, though very near to them, did not oppress their imagination. Their gods were not unknown and dimly felt forces, dwelling in forests, or in solitary places. Through the race of demigods the people traced back their lineage to the Immortals, who mingled in the open ways of the city, in the streets and market-places, and joined in their feasts and graced their solemn meetings.

The companions of their sports, the partners of their revels, these gods accepted the homage of dance and song. They were members of the same family, elder brothers, who inspired a grave reverence, but no servile fear.

On another side, the Greek, combining the gaiety, the insatiable curiosity of the child with the keen intellect of the grown man, went forth fearlessly to explore each undiscovered region that lay around him and within. The joy of adventure carried him over unknown seas; the spirit of daring speculation led him to investigate the world both of matter and of mind, and to embrace in his theories the ultimate constitution of things. The spectacle of the universe with its puzzles and contradictions, and of human life with its mingled pleasures and pains, to each of which appeals his quick sympathies readily responded, left the balance of his faculties undisturbed. From his flights of speculation and fancy he came back to the world of action and lived in it as though he had never left it—shrewd in business, fond of enjoyment, but temperate in his pleasures, scrupulous in the performance of domestic pieties, meeting danger with courage and defeat with resignation. Even in exile he could find a retreat in the serenity of his own thought. "No Hellene is old," said the Egyptian priest in Plato,[1] "in mind you are all young": and we willingly apply the words to the Greeks in a somewhat different sense from what was intended, and think of them as of their own victorious athletes, endowed with perpetual youth and gaiety of heart, with radiant limbs and brows unclouded, the inward and outward man being one in the gracious union of intellect and beauty.

But however true this picture may be if regarded in its main outlines, there is another side to it of which we ought to be reminded. It is not difficult to picture to ourselves some of the sombre facts which dashed the joyousness of Greek life in the periods with which we are best acquainted—the hard and narrow selfishness of the ruling class, the fierce bigotry, the wild revenge of political faction, the sudden reversals of fortune, and the instability of all human affairs. But even if we confine ourselves to literature, and note only the moods and sentiments which are there reflected, we may catch many plaintive tones and some accents even of

[1] Plato, *Tim.* 22 B.

despair, which contrast strangely with what is called Hellenic serenity.

A peculiar vein of constitutional sadness belongs to the Greek temperament. We find it already in Homer. In Achilles himself, as in most of the heroes of poetry, there is a tinge of melancholy. His early death is the burden of the *Iliad.* "Doomed art thou to swift death, yea and piteous art thou above all men; in an evil hour I bare thee in our halls";[1]—so cries Thetis, when at the opening of the *Iliad* she comes at the call of her son; and the same word, *ὠκύμορος*, is on her lips when, after the death of Patroclus, she again answers the same call;[2] and once more in her prayer to Hephaestus to forge new armour for Achilles she pleads for a son that is "doomed to swift death."[3] From his mother Achilles had learnt that he had the choice between two fates. "If I abide here and besiege the Trojans' city, then my returning home is taken from me, but my fame shall be imperishable; but if I go home to my dear native land, my high fame is taken from me, but my life shall endure long while, neither shall the issue of death soon reach me."[4]

[1] *Il.* i. 417. [2] *Il.* xviii. 95. [3] *Il.* xviii. 458.
[4] *Il.* ix. 412-16. Trans. by Leaf, Lang, and Myers.

Before the opening of the *Iliad* the choice has been made. Achilles already knows his doom and accepts it. His one wish is, that seeing that his span of life is brief (*μινυνθάδιόν περ ἐόντα*), it might not be without honour.[1] It is with him as with Hector. The shadow of early death falls across both their paths. "Of a surety," says Hector, "I know this in heart and soul; the day shall come for holy Ilios to be laid low, and Priam and the folk of Priam of the good ashen spear."[2] But not the love of wife or child can make him shrink like a coward from the battle; "seeing I have learnt ever to be valiant and fight in the forefront of the Trojans, winning my father's great glory and mine own."[3]

Still more clearly does Achilles know what is in store for him; and the foreknowledge lends a peculiar pathos to all he says and does. Yet no word escapes him of querulous lament. In his anguish over the death of Patroclus he exclaims: "But bygones will we let be, for all our pain, curbing the heart in our breasts under necessity. Now go I forth, that I may light on the destroyer of him I loved, on Hector: then will I accept my death whensoever Zeus

[1] *Il.* i. 352. [2] *Il.* vi. 447-49. [3] *Il.* vi. 444-46.

willeth to accomplish it and the other immortal gods."[1] One line sums up the spirit of the man: "When I am dead I shall lie low; let me now win high renown."[2] To the horse Xanthus, who being endowed with human speech told him of his death-day nigh at hand, he answered: "Xanthus, why prophesiest thou my death? no wise behoveth it thee. Well know I of myself that it is appointed me to perish here, far from my father dear and mother; howbeit anywise I will not refrain till I give the Trojans surfeit of war."[3] Finally, in the great scene where Priam comes to his tent at night and entreats of him the body of Hector, Achilles is softened by the old man's grief and by his own. He thinks too of his father Peleus to whom the gods gave fortune and wealth, and a bride from among the daughters of the sea. Trouble too they gave, for he "begat one son to an untimely death" (*ἕνα παῖδα τέκεν παναώριον*),[4] a son who may not tend him in old age, but abides far off in Troy land. In this memorable speech,[5] however, he rises above the

[1] *Il.* xviii. 114-16.

[2] *Il.* xviii. 121, *κείσομ' ἐπεί κε θάνω· νῦν δὲ κλέος ἐσθλὸν ἀροίμην.*

[3] *Il.* xix. 420-23.

[4] *Il.* xxiv. 540.

[5] *Il.* xxiv. 518-51.

personal sorrow to the height of human pity, and draws a picture never yet surpassed of human destiny, of the "lot the gods have spun for miserable men."

The strain of sadness in Achilles that here finds its fullest utterance, is a characteristic example of Homer's melancholy. It is large, human, universal. "Even as are the generations of leaves such are those likewise of men; the leaves that the wind scattereth to earth, and the forest budding putteth forth another growth, and the new leaves come on in the spring-tide; so of the generations of men one putteth forth its bloom and another passeth away."[1] These words, the first conscious sigh over the mortality of man that is found in Greek poetry, were spoken by Glaucus to Diomede when the two warriors met in single combat; and again and again in Homer, above the din of battle and the triumph of the victor, is heard the voice of human tenderness, the pathos of suffering. All distinctions are effaced; Greeks and Trojans, friends and foes, are confounded in the deep compassion which the poet feels for the woes and tears of humanity.

[1] *Il.* vi. 146-49. Cp. Ecclesiasticus xiv. 18, "As of the green leaves on a thick tree, some fall, and some grow; so is the generation of flesh and blood, one cometh to an end, and another is born."

But the melancholy of Homer is more akin to the melancholy of youth than of mature age. The mood of sadness follows close upon other moments when the pleasure of existence and the vision of the world's beauty have penetrated and possessed the mind. The two moods are in their nature not so far apart, and by natural reaction pass each into the other. Both spring out of unlimited aspiration, out of a deep thirst and capacity for joy. With riper years the discovery of the disproportion which must always exist between desire and achievement, brings with it a kindly acquiescence in much that is imperfect. The heroic aim of the Homeric men has not yet been brought down to the level of the actual. Still farther are we from the period of middle-aged pessimism when ideals are shattered and all that life offers has been found wanting. But while the poetic melancholy of the early Greek world is not unconnected with the high hopes of youth, to whose untried faculties every effort is in itself a delight, the similarity between the two forms of melancholy is only partial. Youthful melancholy is fantastic and egoistic. It lives in a world of its own and everywhere sees its own image reflected. It is a world of bright day-dreams which melt away and again re-form. When the fabric of hope is dissolved, youth is apt to rebel against the conditions of existence. And even apart from such disappointment, there are seasons when the pain of living becomes almost too keen to be borne; no precise reason can be assigned; it is an instinctive feeling. The melancholy of Homer is free from these fantastic elements. Illusion and disillusion do not succeed one another. With the freshness of youthful life and its boundless capacity of action is combined the quiet and calm gaze of long experience, the "eye that hath kept watch o'er man's mortality."

But however great is the pathos and tenderness of Homer, he is free from the feeling that death after all is better than life. In the description of the future life in the eleventh *Odyssey* it is the suggestion of lost happiness that throws into high relief the pathos of earthly existence. The underworld of Homer is a meagre and ill-furnished world situated at the limits of the far west in a region of perpetual twilight. The life of its inhabitants is a pale image of what they did on earth. Orion, a phantom hunter, chases phantom beasts—the ghosts of "the very beasts that he himself had slain on the lonely hills." Minos still sits in judgment and holds a spectral tribunal.

There is an automatic mimicry of the activities of the upper world. The one reality is the reality of torment. A few great criminals, who have attempted to overpass the limits of existence and to encroach on the divine prerogative, are visited with a punishment consisting in aimless effort or unsatisfied desire. Hades himself is the "hated of the gods," and the souls go down to him lamenting. His land is desolate of joy, tenanted by "strengthless heads," "phantoms of men outworn." "Rather," says Achilles, "would I live above ground as the hireling of another, with a landless man who had no great livelihood, than bear sway among all the dead that be departed."[1]

The contrast between the bliss of the gods who "live at ease" and the troublous lot they have ordained for man, constitutes part of the pathos of human life in Homer. In like manner in the Homeric *Hymn to the Pythian Apollo*, the listening assembly of Olympus is charmed by the voice of the Muses who "sing of the deathless gifts of the gods and the sorrows of men, even all that they endure by the will of the Immortals, living heedless and helpless, nor can they find a cure for death nor a defence against old age."[2] Again, in

[1] *Od.* xi. 489-91.

[2] *Homeric Hymn* ii. 11 ff. [189 ff.].

the *Hymn to Demeter*, when Metanira by a blind act of motherly love rescues her son, as she thinks, from death, but in truth robs him of the immortality which he would otherwise have won, the goddess cries out: "O foolish children of men, that have no wit to discern the doom of coming good or evil."[1] The ignorance, the short-sightedness of men—this note of later tragedy is struck in Greek poetry from the outset. Nor is it bare ignorance that is so pitiful, it is the blindness of a being who seeing sees not, who mistakes the things that should have been for his good. The irony of fancied knowledge is a recurring motive in Greek literature. It is a thought that is made prominent in the Hesiodic version of the legend of Prometheus. The sentence pronounced by Zeus after the theft of fire was that men should henceforth "delight their soul in cherishing that which was their bane."[2] The skill and intelligence they had gained through the Titan was theirs inalienably, but illusion was to follow knowledge as its shadow.

In Hesiod the discord between intention and

[1] *Homeric Hymn* v. 256:

νήϊδες ἄνθρωποι, ἀφράδμονες οὔτ' ἀγάθοιο
αἶσαν ἐπερχομένου προγνώμεναι οὔτε κακοῖο.

[2] Hesiod, *Works and Days*, 58:

τέρπωνται κατὰ θυμὸν ἑὸν κακὸν ἀμφαγαπῶντες.

result is but the final pain added to the misery of man's lot. The whole spectacle of human life is unutterably wretched. The poet has fallen on evil days, on the last and worst age of a world that is degenerating. Diseases, silent and voiceless,[1] hover round mortals and assail them : "never by day shall they cease from toil and sorrow, or in the night-time from destruction."[2] In one comprehensive lament the immense wretchedness of humanity is summed up : "The earth is full of woes, and full also the sea."[3] Yet he asserts the moral government of the universe ; there is no accent of revolt against the gods. He bows to their decree, simply because it is inevitable, and preaches the lesson of work. Work is the one road to excellence : the way is long and steep, and at first is hard ; but it grows easier as you gain the summit.[4] "There is no shame in labour : idleness is shame."[5] The inducements to work are frankly

[1] Hesiod, *Works and Days*, 104 :

σιγῇ, ἐπεὶ φωνὴν ἐξείλετο μητίετα Ζεύς.

[2] *Ib.* 173 :

οὐδέ ποτ' ἦμαρ
παύσονται καμάτου καὶ ὀϊζύος οὐδέ τι νύκτωρ
φθειρόμενοι.

[3] *Ib.* 101, πλείη μὲν γὰρ γαῖα κακῶν, πλείη δὲ θάλασσα.

[4] *Ib.* 287-90.

[5] *Ib.* 309, ἔργον δ' οὐδὲν ὄνειδος, ἀεργίη δέ τ' ὄνειδος.

stated ; they are merely the satisfaction of material wants, and the need of escaping from the intolerable conditions of an effortless existence. But the spirit and tone in which Hesiod develops his precepts rise to a higher level ; as he unfolds them one by one labour becomes more than a sad necessity : it adds dignity to life ; nay, it yields a pleasure of its own. Hesiod is not at heart one of those to whom existence is a burden. He feels the glow that comes from obstacles vanquished and from energy of will. His deep compassion for mankind does not prevent him from clinging fondly to the few simple joys that are within the reach of man.

Another and more modern phase of melancholy is not slow to find expression in Greek poetry. In Mimnermus, who wrote in the middle of the seventh century B.C., we see the Greek spirit aged, as it were, before its day. The few fragments of him that have been preserved are all written in one strain. His theme is the fleeting delights of youth that passes away like a dream, and old age, loveless and joyless, "hateful to children, scorned by women," which "makes beauty and ugliness to be alike," and "in the sunlight find no pleasure." He moralises sadly upon life ; and while his tone is one of reflective resignation, the conclusion to which he points is that man's wisdom is to snatch the pleasures of the hour. He takes as his text the Homeric lines quoted above[1]—

οἵηπερ φύλλων γενεή, τοίη δὲ καὶ ἀνδρῶν κ.τ.λ.

lines which are among the favourite reminiscences of the elegiac poets—and expands the idea; but how far has he travelled from the simple thought of Homer! "We are like leaves which the flowering spring-time brings forth, when of a sudden they grow beneath the rays of the sun; for a span so brief do we rejoice in the flowers of youth, knowing nothing, neither good nor evil, from the gods. But the black fates stand by, the one with the doom of doleful age, the other with the doom of death; and for a little space the fruit of youth continues, during one day's sunshine on the earth. But when once the appointed time of youth is passed, better to die forthwith than to live."[2]

Theognis, too, who lived nearly a century later, is, like Mimnermus, a practical Epicurean: "I rejoice and disport me in my youth; long enough beneath the earth shall I lie, bereft of life, voice-

[1] *Supr.* p. 139.

[2] Mimnerm. Fr. 2.

less as a stone, and shall leave the loved sunlight; good man though I am, then shall I see nothing any more."[1] "Rejoice, O my soul, in thy youth; soon shall other men be in life, and I shall be black earth in death."[2] "After my death I crave not to be laid upon a royal couch; nay, in life may some luck be mine. Briars for the dead man are as coverlets strewn over him. What if the bed be hard or soft?"[3] Life has not gone so smoothly with Theognis as with Mimnermus. He has been engaged in the political struggles of his own city Megara, and is the victim of social revolution; he has been in exile, has lost his fortune, has been deserted by friends: he knows what it is to have the spirit tongue-tied, to be broken and enslaved by poverty.[4] And, though now again he is restored to his country, an accent of personal emotion, a sharp sense of wrong, vibrates through his verses, and with it there is a passionate longing to be avenged and "to drink the black blood" of his enemies.[5] He looks out upon the world and sees everywhere a reign of lawlessness and violence: "Shame has perished; shamelessness and outrage have conquered justice,

[1] Theogn. 567-70. [2] *Ib.* 877-78. [3] *Ib.* 1191-94.
[4] *Ib.* 177-78. [5] *Ib.* 349.

and prevail throughout the world."[1] The greed of wealth has levelled all distinctions of birth and blood;[2] "those who once were noble now are base, and the base in turn are noble."[3] Seeing that it avails nothing to be just, let a man be cunning and shifty, and imitate the polypus which takes the colour of the rock to which it clings.[4] The cry which escapes him—

ὄλβιος οὐδεὶς
ἀνθρώπων, ὁπόσους ἠέλιος καθορᾷ—[5]

"No mortal is happy of all on whom the sun looks down," is a more genuine lamentation than is often conveyed by these well-worn words in the Greek poets. His despair reaches its height in the famous lines whose echoes lived long in Greek literature: "It is best of all things for the children of men not to be born, nor to see the rays of the keen sunlight; but if born, to pass as soon as may be the gates of Hades, and to lie beneath a vesture of much earth."[6]

[1] Theogn. 291-92. [2] *Ib.* 190. [3] *Ib.* 1109-10.
[4] *Ib.* 215-16. [5] *Ib.* 167-68.
[6] *Ib.* 425-28:

πάντων μὲν μὴ φῦναι ἐπιχθονίοισιν ἄριστον,
μηδ' ἐσιδεῖν αὐγὰς ὀξέος ἠελίου.
φύντα δ', ὅπως ὤκιστα πύλας 'Αΐδαο περῆσαι,
καὶ κεῖσθαι πολλὴν γῆν ἐπαμησάμενον.

Cp. Soph. *O. C.* 1225:

Yet Theognis with studied self-control teaches the wisdom which he has learnt as a child,[1] and endeavours to guide the friend whom he addresses in the ancient ways. The thoughts of man's heart are vain; he knows nothing of the issue whether for good or evil, for the gods ordain all things as they will.[2] Man must humble himself before the gods and take cheerfully the evil things of life as well as the good.[3] Yet now and again while repeating the maxims of piety he suddenly breaks off, overcome by the thought of the sufferings of the righteous; he turns to Zeus and charges him with injustice in his government of the world in language almost as bold as that of the *Prometheus* of Aeschylus, or of the *Book of Job*: "Zeus, lord beloved, I marvel at thee; for thou reignest over all; thine is honour and great power, and thou knowest the very heart and spirit of each man,

---

μὴ φῦναι τὸν ἅπαντα νικᾷ λόγον· τὸ δ', ἐπεὶ φανῇ,
βῆναι κεῖθεν ὅθενπερ ἥκει πολὺ δεύτερον ὡς τάχιστα.

Eur. Fr. 900 (Nauck):

τὸ μὴ γενέσθαι κρεῖσσον ἢ φῦναι βροτοῖς.

Cp. also Bacchyl. Fr. 3. So Ecclesiastes iv. 2, 3, "I praised the dead which are already dead, more than the living which are yet alive. Yea, better is he than both they, which hath not yet been."

[1] Theogn. 27-28. [2] *Ib.* 133-42. [3] *Ib.* 335-38.

for thy might, O king, is supreme. How then, son of Cronos, can thy soul endure to hold in like regard the sinner and the righteous? . . . Heaven has given to mortals no clear token, nor shown the way by which if a man walk he may please the Immortals. Howbeit the wicked prosper and are free from trouble, while those who keep their soul from base deeds, although they love justice have for their portion poverty, poverty mother of helplessness, which tempts the mind of man to transgression, and by a cruel constraint mars the reason in his breast." [1]

Solon had consoled himself with the reflection that the works of outrage are not lasting; that Zeus surveys the end, and that of a sudden his vengeance bursts forth, like a wind in spring-time scattering the clouds. Sooner or later it falls, if not on the guilty man himself, on his children and on their posterity after them.[2] Theognis finds no comfort in this thought; rather it heightens the wrong of which he complains. He prays to Zeus that it may be the will of the blessed gods to redress this injustice, that the guilty one may not escape while another bears the penalty, and that the sins of the father may not be visited on the

[1] Theogn. 373-86. [2] Solon, Fr. 13. [4.] 14-32.

sons. As it is, he asks, how can any one, who beholds the afflictions of the righteous and the prosperity of the unjust, henceforth revere the Immortals?[1] Theognis comes as near as a Greek of the earlier time well can come to being a pessimist. At bottom he has a profound conviction, born probably of bitter and personal disappointment, that the world as now ordered is all wrong. He appeals to Zeus to right it; he does not indeed discard the moral precepts and traditional beliefs of his countrymen, but behind these phrases there is no real assurance that the goodness of Zeus is equal to his power: there is little hope that the contradictions which present themselves to the reason will ever be removed.

We pass from Theognis to another and immeasurably greater poet, Pindar, who also felt profoundly the sadness of human destiny, but expressed the feeling in a truly Hellenic spirit. The mortality of man, which to us has become a commonplace of religion or morality, inspired some of the simplest and noblest verses in Greek literature. "Creatures of a day, what are we, what are we not? Man is but a dream of a shadow" (σκιᾶς

[1] Theogn. 731-52.

ὄναρ ἄνθρωπος), says Pindar[1] in an ode which a scholiast calls "a lamentation upon human life." "The dream of a shadow"—that is the starting-point of Pindar's meditations upon man and his destiny. Man, a thing of naught, is not of the lineage of the gods,[2] who know neither weariness nor sickness nor old age;[3] who can speedily accomplish all that they resolve, who can turn darkness to light and light to darkness;[4] from whom no mortal deed is hidden.[5] But as for men, the gods deal to them two evils for one good;[6] their delight grows up apace, but as quickly it falls again to earth.[7] Errors unnumbered float around their thought.[8]

Yet man, frail and feeble, has a light that springs from him in the darkness. "When a glory from God hath shined on him a clear light abideth upon him, and serene life."[9] He wins to his side Fortune—not the fickle goddess, who with closed eyes distributes her bounties, and raises men up only to cast them down, but Fortune, the Saviour (τύχη Σώτειρα),[10] who works in harmony with the

[1] *Pyth.* viii. 95. Trans. by E. Myers.
[2] *Nem.* vi. 1-4.
[3] Fr. Inc. 120 [127], Bergk.
[4] *Ib.* 119 [106].
[5] *Ol.* i. 64.
[6] *Pyth.* iii. 81.
[7] *Ib.* viii. 92-94.
[8] *Ol.* vii. 24-25.
[9] *Pyth.* viii. 96-97.
[10] *Ol.* xii. 2.

moral powers which sustain the world. Thus the "short-lived race of man" (*τὸ ταχύποτμον ἀνέρων ἔθνος*)[1] may struggle and do battle for what is noble.[2] "Never indeed shall man climb the brazen heaven,"[3] yet he has in him some likeness to the Immortals.[4] Youth, beauty, victorious strength, fair deeds made immortal by song—these are god-given gifts and in these the crown of human glory is attained. But the just man only is beloved of the gods; in life he is under their protection, and in death too a new hope is given him. Perpetual sunlight has arisen upon the realm of the shades; fair meadow-lands bloom where Homer knew only of barren trees that shed their fruit. A more full and conscious existence opens out after death, and the world below is brought into moral relation with the life on earth.[5] Pindar's vein of meditation is free from despair or pessimism. His grave melancholy has nothing in it that is unmanly. He remains a Hellene of the Hellenes. The singer of the games, the poet of a privileged race of athletes, who by birth and wealth and native faculty were able

[1] *Ol.* i. 66.
[2] *Ib.* v. 15; cp. *Nem.* v. 47.
[3] *Pyth.* x. 27.
[4] *Nem.* vi. 4.
[5] *Ol.* ii. 53-83, Fr. 106 [95], 108 [96].

to rise to the level of heroic achievement, he is not forgetful of the vanity of human hopes, of man's nothingness and entire dependence on the gods.

The impressions made on the greater poets by the contemplation of life have their counterpart in the thought, prematurely aged, of the "weeping philosopher" of Greece. Heraclitus, the lofty and disdainful spirit,[1] who stood aloof from the vulgar, wrote over the passing phenomena of existence the words, *πάντα χωρεῖ καὶ οὐδὲν μένει*,[2] "all things give place; nothing is permanent." He was the first, by a sad philosophy, to break up the solid foundations of the universe, and to see everywhere an endless tide of change, a perpetually dissolving view. The same sense of instability and vicissitude is manifest in the writings of the historians, and in them becomes penetrated with poetic feeling. For, in truth, the facts of Greek history were instinct with poetry. As the poetry of Greece was more historical than that of any other people, so too its history was more poetical. Already to a Greek of the fifth century B.C. the law of moral retribution was written legibly on the page of the past. Events had unfolded themselves with

[1] Diog. Laert. ix. 1, *μεγαλόφρων δὲ γέγονε παρ' ὁντιναοῦν καὶ ὑπερόπτης*.

[2] Plat. *Crat.* 402 A.

startling rapidity; signal catastrophes gave emphasis to what was happening; causes and effects, which in a more complicated modern society are hard to disentangle, stood out in their clear meaning and their inevitable issues. In a single century, 620 to 520 B.C., five great empires—Assyria, Media, Babylonia, Lydia, Egypt—had passed away with every circumstance of dramatic impressiveness; a still shorter period had witnessed the rise and fall of the Tyrannies in Greece. In an age when the despot of to-day might to-morrow be an exile, when the triumph of political party meant frequently not only loss of power and place, but of home and property, and, it might be, of life for the vanquished—at such a time the poet and the historian could draw from a common inspiration. Greek history was a living witness to the deeper laws which govern human action: Greek tragedy became an epitome of the lessons of Greek history, the facts of the mythical past being read in the light of contemporary reflection.

Dramatic surprises and a Divine Irony in the ordering of events—these were the great ideas common to Herodotus (in some measure even to Thucydides) and the tragedians. In applying these ideas to life marked discrepancies of thought and treatment are apparent. But in all alike great disasters are seen to follow close upon insolent success; man's fancied security is the prelude to his fall. Like Aeschylus, Herodotus looks behind the natural causes of events and finds a divine hand that guides them. The gods are guardians of right: crime brings its sure penalties: its consequences extend to generations yet unborn. The connexion between sin and suffering, which in Aeschylus is exhibited in the hereditary doom of certain families, Herodotus traces on the larger stage of the world's history and in the life of nations. While he thus resembles Aeschylus as the exponent of the law of Nemesis, he also recalls Sophocles in the recurring thought of the briefness of the individual life and the insecurity of mortal happiness. Few and evil are the days of man's existence, he lives in a vain shadow, unable to forecast his future, and feeding upon idle hopes. In the hour when he seems to have attained, failure and catastrophe are already at hand. One last pain there is even worse than ignorance—to unite perfect knowledge with perfect helplessness.[1]

[1] Her. ix. 16, πολλὰ φρονέοντα μηδενὸς κρατέειν.

It may appear a paradox to speak of the melancholy of Herodotus; and indeed it would be so if the word is taken to imply a gloomy or pessimistic temperament. His history overflows with natural gaiety. He has moreover a reasoned confidence in the general ordering of human affairs; and as he relates the great deeds of his race in the overthrow of the armies of Persia, his heart, as a Hellene, glows with pride. Still there is in him a strain of manly and resigned melancholy, a side of his character which is not out of keeping with his joy-loving nature. Almost at the opening of his history he writes as one who has read the story of human vicissitudes and has been a close spectator of existence. There is a tone of grave reflection in the words: "I will tell of the cities of men, small as well as great; for those which once were great have for the most part become small; and those which in my time were great were small of old. Knowing then that human prosperity never continues in one stay, I shall make mention of things small and great alike."[1] When he tells of the tears of Xerxes, as from his throne at Abydos he watched his countless hosts passing into Europe,

[1] Her. i. 5.

and reflected that in a hundred years not one of those multitudes would be living, we feel that these are the very tears that Greek tragedy evokes: this is the tragic pity or ἔλεος, which in the woes of the individual laments the universal human destiny. In a similar strain of profound compassion the chorus in the *Oedipus Tyrannus*, on finding out the secret of Oedipus' birth, exclaims, "Alas, ye generations of men, how mere a shadow do I count your life. Where, where is the mortal who wins more of happiness than just the seeming, and after the semblance a falling away?" [1]

This, which is the dominant mood of Sophocles, is heard as an undertone throughout the narrative of Herodotus. It is but rarely put into so many words, but when it does find utterance it is in accents that betray a profound disquiet of which Sophocles knows nothing. Sophocles was able to look on the world in the resigned temper of religious faith, and to see its contradictions reconciled in a moral harmony by a supreme and righteous will, which has regard even for the individual life. Herodotus trusts indeed in the general course of providence, but for him there

[1] Soph. *O. T.* 1186-92. Trans. by R. C. Jebb.

are still unharmonised forces in the universe, which assail human happiness. A jealous power gives to man a taste of the sweets of life only to withdraw the cup from his lips. So full of trouble is life that death is the most acceptable refuge from its ills. "Short as our life is," said the Persian Artabanus to Xerxes, "there is no mortal so happy that he will not many times, and not once only, have occasion to wish that he were dead rather than alive."[1]

Yet Herodotus is neither despairing nor defiant. His attitude of practical piety is not very different from that of Sophocles. From the facts of life poet and historian alike draw the same lesson, that a mortal man must not strive to rise above mortal estate, but must bear humbly the lot that is decreed for him. In Herodotus too there are already hints of the thought concisely expressed in the saying of Heraclitus, "It is not well for man to win all that he desires" (*ἀνθρώποισι γίνεσθαι ὁκόσα θέλουσι οὐκ ἄμεινον*),—a thought more fully developed by Sophocles. Man does not know his own true good; what seems to be his ruin may be his saving; for there are divine-sent visitations which reveal a providential

[1] Her. vii. 46.

purpose. Croesus, the deposed monarch, learns a wisdom hidden from him in prosperity: not Oedipus, the king, who solved the riddle of the Sphinx, but Oedipus, the blind man and the wanderer, is admitted to the secrets of the gods. Of all boons death itself may be the best; as for the two Argive youths, Cleobis and Biton, who drew their mother to the temple of Hera, and when in sight of all the people she had prayed to the goddess to grant them the best thing which man can receive, they fell asleep and rose no more.[1]

The abiding sense of man's helplessness and of the mystery of his fate accounts for the peculiar tone in which Hope is spoken of in Greek literature. There is one notable exception in the *Prometheus* of Aeschylus. The "blind hopes" which Prometheus planted in men's minds helped them to emerge out of a feeble and grovelling life, and to rise above the thought of death.[2] Many minor examples may be found of Hope in this happier aspect.[3] But it is more commonly pictured as a flattering phantom, an illusion born of an uncertain future. It is a mocking

[1] Her. I. 31.

[2] *Prom.* 248-51.

[3] *E.g.* Pind. *Isth.* vii. 16, Fr. 198 [233]. Eur. *Herc. Fur.* 105-106. Theogn. 1143-46. Dem. *de Cor.* § 97. The phrase ἀγαθὴ or ἡδεῖα ἐλπίς has often a special reference to hopes after death.

goddess who tempts men to forget the limits of the possible. It is the consolation of the weak, whom it lures to folly; it is not a spur to progress nor the sustenance of the strong. In Hesiod, when the lid was removed from Pandora's jar, and the other myriad evils which it contained flew abroad, Hope alone remained at the bottom—itself, too, part of the deadly gift of the goddess. In Theognis, Hope and Peril stand near to one another, both of them dangerous deities to man.[1] In Pindar "up and down the hopes of men are tossed, as they cleave the waves of baffling falsity."[2] "By hope unconscionable our bodies are enthralled; but the tides of foresight lie afar."[3] To Pindar also the saying is by some ascribed: "Hopes are the dreams of waking men."[4] In Simonides of Amorgos it is Hope that supports man in his vain endeavours after the unattainable; meanwhile old age, disease, and death overtake him.[5] In Thucydides, Hope is the strength of the desperate and is contrasted with the foresight which comes of reason.[6] Once more, it is the

[1] Theogn. 637-38.
[2] *Ol.* xii. 5.
[3] *Nem.* xi. 45.
[4] Stob. iii. 12.
[5] Simon. Amorg. Fr. 1 (Bergk).
[6] Thuc. ii. 62, 5, ἐλπίδι τε ἧσσον πιστεύει, ἧς ἐν τῷ ἀπόρῳ ἡ ἰσχύς, γνώμῃ δὲ ἀπὸ τῶν ὑπαρχόντων, ἧς βεβαιοτέρα ἡ πρόνοια.

ruinous adviser, the spendthrift counsellor who prompts men to stake their all, and is detected only when all has been lost;[1] a sentiment placed with characteristic dramatic effect in the mouth of the Athenians just before the Sicilian expedition, in which the contrast between the hope and the fulfilment reaches to the height of tragic irony. In the Greek Anthology, Hope and Fortune are two companion goddesses who make a sport of human life.[2] The future indeed hung like a heavy cloud over the ancient world, charged with catastrophes, reversals of fortune, the wreck of states, the breaking up of homes, exile and death. In the face of these uncertainties the virtue of the Greeks was Resignation rather than Hope, a cheerful acceptance (*στέργειν*) of the gods' will, without any joyful or assured anticipations.

In Greek authors of classical times there is no trace of the thought that the human race as a whole, or any single people, is advancing towards a divinely appointed goal; there is nothing of

[1] Thuc. v. 103, *τοῖς δ' ἐς ἅπαν τὸ ὕπαρχον ἀναρριπτοῦσι (δάπανος γὰρ φύσει) ἅμα τε γιγνώσκεται σφαλέντων, καὶ κ.τ.λ.*

[2] *Anth. Pal.* ix. 49:

> Ἐλπὶς καὶ σὺ Τύχη, μέγα χαίρετε· τὸν λιμέν' εὗρον·
> οὐδὲν ἐμοί χ' ὑμῖν· παίζετε τοὺς μετ' ἐμέ.

So ix. 134, 172; x. 70.

what the moderns mean by the "Education of the World," "the Progress of the Race," "the Divine guidance of Nations." The first germ of the thought is in Polybius (*circ.* 204-122 B.C.), whose work illustrates the idea of a providential destiny presiding over the march of Roman history, and building up the imperial power of Rome for the good of mankind. Diodorus Siculus (*circ.* 59 B.C.), again, speaks of the gratitude due to those historians who, seeing men bound together by natural kinship but separated in place and time, have attempted to bring them together in one ordered whole (*ὑπὸ μίαν καὶ τὴν αὐτὴν σύνταξιν ἀγαγεῖν*), therein making themselves the ministers of Divine Providence (*ὥσπερ τινὲς ὑπουργοὶ τῆς θείας προνοίας γενηθέντες*).[1] The notion of a universal history is here based on the sentiment of the unity of the human race and of its hopes for the future.

Greek thought turned mainly to the past. The Greek orators and political writers drew their inspiration either from mythical heroes or from the achievements of their ancestors. The Utopias sketched in the comic fragments—the *βίος ἀρχαῖος* or primitive life of innocence — were

[1] Diodor. Sic. i. 1.

placed in a far-off golden age, and consisted in the simple bliss of barbarism. Philosophy, too, was in Aristotle's phrase "fond of myth";[1] it sought out ancient traditions, the fragments of forgotten learning;[2] for, as he maintained, all the arts and sciences have been found and lost again not once but an infinite number of times already.[3] Greek political ideals reflect the prevalent distrust of the future. Plato indeed did not share Aristotle's disbelief in continuous progress; none the less he is well-nigh hopeless for the mass of mankind. Deeply corrupt in all its parts, society does what it can to debase the noblest of its members. The only chance of regenerating it lies in subjecting it to the rule of the philosophers, but hitherto it has listened only to those who have humoured its appetites.

In the absence of Hope and of an ideal of progress, we strike upon one great difference

[1] Arist. *Met.* i. 2. 982 b 18.

[2] *Met.* xi. 8. 1074 b 10-13, καὶ κατὰ τὸ εἰκὸς πολλάκις εὑρημένης εἰς τὸ δυνατὸν ἑκάστης καὶ τέχνης καὶ φιλοσοφίας καὶ πάλιν φθειρομένων καὶ ταύτας τὰς δόξας (*sc.* νομίσειεν ἄν τις) οἷον λείψανα περισεσῶσθαι μέχρι τοῦ νῦν.

[3] *de Caelo* i. 3. 270 b 16-20 . . . οὐ γὰρ ἅπαξ οὐδὲ δὶς ἀλλ' ἀπειράκις δεῖ νομίζειν τὰς αὐτὰς ἀφικνεῖσθαι δόξας εἰς ἡμᾶς. Cp. *Pol.* ii. 5. 1264 a 1-5. iv. (vii.) 10. 1329 b 25-27.

between the classical Greeks and the Hebrews. Not that the history of the Hebrews was one of progressive expansion and orderly development. It was so in a far less degree than that of the Hellenes, being in truth a long record of ever-recurring rebellions and late repentances. The nation was of all others the most full of inner contradictions; the higher and the lower self were never reconciled. Yet in the darkest hour of adversity the Prophets did not despair of Israel. When Jerusalem was desolate, when the people was in captivity, and national existence had been crushed, the voice of prophecy speaks out the more confidently. It recalls the divine guidance that had watched over the race, and tells of the mighty destiny that was in store for Israel. Through the prophets an ideal and glorified national sentiment was created, transcending local limits, and intertwined with the highest hopes that could be conceived for humanity. They looked to a spiritual restoration and triumph, which should be for the world at large the beginning of a glorious future. This ideal, ardently desired, possessed the mind of the pious Jew: it fed in him a sacred fund of joy, and kept alive a spark of hope in a world of spiritual despair against the day when He who was "the Desire of all nations" should come.

I shall not attempt to touch, even briefly, on all the phases of melancholy that may be discovered in Greek literature; we are dealing merely with a few typical authors. But Euripides is a poet who ought not to be passed over even in this rapid survey. All tradition represents him as one who took a sombre view of life. His Greek biographer describes him as an austere man (*στρυφνός*), hating laughter (*μισόγελως*), and hating women (*μισογύνης*). It is never indeed very safe to take isolated quotations from a play, and argue from them to the writer's own beliefs. Even such impressive lines as that of Sophocles:

> οὐδὲν γὰρ ἄλγος οἷον ἡ πολλὴ ζόη—[1]

and of Menander:

> ἆρ' ἐστὶ συγγενές τι λύπη καὶ βίος;—[2]

might not, if taken in their context, carry the full weight of sad and personal conviction which we read in them when they stand alone. Euripides, however, holds a somewhat exceptional position. His tendency is to disregard dramatic proprieties,

[1] Soph. Fr. 509 (Nauck).
[2] Menand. Κιθαριστ. Fr. 1.

and to let his own voice be heard behind that of his characters. By the mouth even of women, slaves, and peasants he utters those sententious sayings in which we recognise the poet's generalised experience. We must be careful, of course, not to find too much significance in such individual utterances, or to lose sight of the necessary one-sidedness inherent in all compendious maxims about life. We have no need, however, in this instance to rely on particular expressions: the poetic thought of Euripides is saturated with a profound feeling for human suffering, human ignorance, human infirmity. In him, if anywhere in Greek tragedy, *Sunt lacrimae rerum.* The total impression left on us by his plays is that the temperament of the writer is as far as possible removed from "Greek gaiety of heart." The fragments of Euripides, remarkable, in spite of their variety, for a pervading unity of tone, reinforce this general impression. At the best "the life of wretched mortals is not wholly fortunate or wholly luckless, but blessed and then again unblessed."[1] It is chequered with sunshine and

[1] Eur. Fr. 196 (Nauck):

τοίοσδε θνητῶν τῶν ταλαιπώρων βίος·
οὔτ' εὐτυχεῖ τὸ πάμπαν οὔτε δυστυχεῖ,
εὐδαιμονεῖ δὲ καὖθις οὐκ εὐδαιμονεῖ.

shade, as changing as the seasons of the year.[1] In past happiness there is no pledge of the future: "For somehow the god, if god he must be called, grows weary of consorting always with the same folk."[2] Yet mortals, burdened with countless ills, still love life; they long for each coming day, glad to bear the thing they know rather than face death, the unknown.[3]

There is little doubt that at one time at least Euripides was profoundly troubled as to the moral ordering of the world. In later years, however, he seems to have attained a speculative calm. The injustice we ascribe to the gods is, he thinks, rather the confusion wrought by man.[4] There is a divine justice which works itself out: yet not, it may be, in the individual life, but

[1] Eur. Fr. 332 (Nauck).

[2] *Ib.* 1058:

> ὁ γὰρ θεός πως, εἰ θεόν σφε χρὴ καλεῖν,
> κάμνει ξυνὼν τὰ πολλὰ τοῖς αὐτοῖς ἀεί.

[3] *Ib.* 813:

> ὦ φιλόζωοι βροτοί,
> οἳ τὴν ἐπιστείχουσαν ἡμέραν ἰδεῖν
> ποθεῖτ', ἔχοντες μυρίων ἄχθος κακῶν.
> οὕτως ἔρως βροτοῖσιν ἔγκειται βίου.
> τὸ ζῆν γὰρ ἴσμεν· τοῦ θανεῖν δ' ἀπειρίᾳ
> πᾶς τις φοβεῖταί φῶς λιπεῖν τόδ' ἡλίου.

[4] *Ib.* 609:

> οὐκ ἔστι τὰ θεῶν ἄδικ', ἐν ἀνθρώποισι δὲ
> κακοῖς νοσοῦντα σύγχυσιν πολλὴν ἔχει.

slowly, and in the long course of human destiny.[1] Towards this conclusion his reason tends; but it never acquires the force of a living conviction; and the religious consolations, therefore, which supported the older tragedians are not to be looked for in him. The end of the *Hercules Furens* presents an interesting contrast to that of the *Oedipus Coloneus*. In both plays the hero has held out to him the promise of consecration after death; but while Oedipus accepts it as full amends for all he has suffered, Hercules rejects with disdain the similar offer of Theseus. Again, in Aeschylus and Sophocles it may fairly be said that the most tragic endings leave a sense of final triumph, or at least of justice vindicated; but even the happy endings of Euripides stir anxious questionings and reveal some inward conflict or misgiving. We must be on our guard, however, not unduly to deepen the shadows which are cast across his tragedies. The tangled skein of existence perplexes him, it is true; but no settled gloom, much less despair, broods over his spirit. He looks out upon the heights of a serene wisdom that may be won by human reason; above all, he has faith in the efficacy of

[1] Cp. *Bacch.* 882. Fr. 969.

human fortitude. High courage (εὐψυχία) is with him the primary virtue in as real a sense as piety (εὐσέβεια) is with Sophocles.

A word remains to be said about those exquisite gems of verse which are contained in the Greek Anthology. Many moods are there reflected. The lines are sometimes bright and playful, sometimes pathetic, sometimes cynical, always graceful. But the motto which is written on the pages as a whole is the same as that of the book of Ecclesiastes, "Vanity of Vanities"—ματαιότης ματαιοτήτων—and the dominant note of sadness deepens the farther we follow the poems into Roman times. "All is laughter, all is ashes, all is nothingness."[1] "Weeping I was born, having wept my fill I die: tears in plenty have I found through life."[2] "Naked I came upon earth, naked shall I go below; why then do I toil in vain; seeing that the end is nakedness?"[3] "Life is the plaything of Fortune,

[1] *Anth. Pal.* x. 124:

πάντα γέλως καὶ πάντα κόνις καὶ πάντα τὸ μηδέν.

[2] *Ib.* x. 84:

δακρυχέων γενόμην, καὶ δακρύσας ἀποθνήσκω·
δάκρυσι δ' ἐν πολλοῖς τὸν βίον εὗρον ὅλον.

[3] *Ib.* x. 58:

γῆς ἐπέβην γυμνός, γυμνός θ' ὑπὸ γαῖαν ἄπειμι·
καὶ τί μάτην μοχθῶ, γυμνὸν ὁρῶν τὸ τέλος;

a piteous thing, a wanderer, tossed to and fro between poverty and wealth."[1] Herodotus (v. 4) tells us of a Thracian tribe, whose custom it was to wail over the birth of a child, and to bury the dead with festive joy, as being released from their troubles. "Let us praise the Thracians," says a writer in the Anthology,[2] "in that they mourn for their sons as they come forth from their mother's womb into the sunlight, while those again they count blessed who have left life, snatched away by Doom unseen, the servant of the Fates." One who had looked upon the course of the world and the treacherous ways of fortune is forced to exclaim: "I hate the world for its mystery."[3]

In such a world how should man order his life? The answers are various, but may be resolved mainly into two—the choice being tersely

[1] *Anth. Pal.* x. 80:

> παίγνιόν ἐστι Τύχης μερόπων βίος, οἰκτρός, ἀλήτης,
> πλούτου καὶ πενίης μεσσόθι ῥεμβόμενος.

[2] *Ib.* ix. 111. Cp. Eur. Fr. 452 (Nauck):

> ἐχρῆν γὰρ ἡμᾶς σύλλογον ποιουμένους
> τὸν φύντα θρηνεῖν εἰς ὅσ' ἔρχεται κακά,
> τὸν δ' αὖ θανόντα καὶ πόνων πεπαυμένον
> χαίροντας εὐφημοῦντας ἐκπέμπειν δόμων.

Also *Hamlet*, Act i. Sc. 2:

> "With mirth in funeral, and with dirge in marriage."

[3] *Ib.* x. 96:

> μισῶ τὰ πάντα τῆς ἀδηλίας χάριν.

put thus: "The world is all a stage, life is a sport: away with earnest and learn to play the game, or bear thy pains."[1] "To play the game" means to drain the cup of pleasure, though death, lurking in the chalice, embitters the dregs. "Nay, come prepare me the joyous stream of Bacchus, for that is the antidote of ills"—forms the conclusion to an epigram which begins by asking, "How was I born? whence am I? wherefore came I hither? To go hence again."[2] On the other hand, to refuse to play the game is to rebel against life, either by way of cynical protest or of sullen submission; and the end should be an early escape from life, if only there might be an escape without dying. To be and not to be, however, are both equally distasteful to the true pessimist; he hates the one, he shrinks from the other. Accordingly we find many exhortations in the Anthology (*e.g.* x. 69) not to fear death, which gives peace, which brings release from sickness and the pains of poverty, which comes once and never comes again.

The minds of nobler temper in the Anthology suffer from something akin to the modern "Welt-

[1] *Anth. Pal.* x. 72:

σκήνη πᾶς ὁ βίος καὶ παίγνιον· ἢ μάθε παίζειν
τὴν σπουδὴν μεταθείς, ἢ φέρε τὰς ὀδύνας.

[2] *Ib.* x. 118.

schmerz," a feeling in which the mystery of life and the sense of the infinite mingle with personal weariness or satiety. Such poets console themselves by singing in charming verse of graves and ruins; of the fallen grandeur of ancient cities—Troy, Mycenae, Argos, Sparta, Corinth; they dwell on the sorrow of remembered happiness, and linger over an ideal or vanished past. In the outer world they find a counterpart to their own moods, or more often still they hear a discord. The placid existence of the cicala or some other member of the animal creation is set off against the restless discontent of man. The sentiment of melancholy blends with a new and almost modern appreciation of nature. Her unchanging majesty is contrasted with man's transient and unquiet energies; to nature the poet turns for support and sympathy. The only sights worth seeing are the larger aspects of the universe around us. "Pleasant are the fair things of nature—earth, sea, stars, the orbs of moon and sun. All else is fearfulness and pain."[1]

[1] *Anth. Pal.* ix. 123:

ἡδέα μὲν γάρ σου τὰ φύσει καλά, γαῖα, θάλασσα,
  ἄστρα, σεληναίης κύκλα καὶ ἠελίου,
τἄλλα δὲ πάντα φόβοι τε καὶ ἄλγεα· κἤν τι πάθῃ τις
  ἐσθλόν, ἀμοιβαίην ἐνδέχεται Νέμεσιν.

If it is true, as Aristotle says,[1] that men of genius are of a melancholy temperament, it is but natural that the most highly gifted nation of antiquity should have had in it a vein of this sentiment. But it would leave a wholly false impression if the word "melancholy," as applied to the representative poets of the Hellenic race, were understood to suggest that for the Greeks there was a keener pleasure to be won from sights and thoughts of gloom than from anything else; that the "sweetest songs are those that tell of saddest thought." We must not lose sight of the distinction between the sadness, which runs as an under-current of thought through the great Greek writers, and the weariness of living which proclaims itself in the graceful and fugitive utterances of the Anthology. Of the various forms of pessimism which we know from literature or life, one form is resigned, so long as its daily allowance of pleasure

---

Cp. the splendid lines of Menander, Ὑποβολιμαῖος, Fr. 2:

τοῦτον εὐτυχέστατον λέγω,
ὅστις θεωρήσας ἀλύπως, Παρμένων,
τὰ σεμνὰ ταῦτ' ἀπῆλθεν, ὅθεν ἦλθεν, ταχύ,
τὸν ἥλιον τὸν κοινόν, ἄστρ', ὕδωρ, νέφη,
πῦρ· ταῦτα, κἂν ἑκατὸν ἔτη βιῷς, ἀεὶ
ὄψει παρόντα, κἂν ἐνιαυτοὺς σφόδρ' ὀλίγους,
σεμνότερα τούτων ἕτερα δ' οὐκ ὄψει ποτέ.

[1] Arist. *Probl.* xxx. 953 a 10 *sqq.*

is not withheld. There is another kind that is scornful, rebellious, imperious in its demands. Examples of both may be found in the Anthology. The older writers with rare exceptions are strangers to both moods. They wait indeed "to see the end"; they will "call no man happy before he dies." Their melancholy is very real, but there is no parade of melancholy. They are not like the "young gentlemen of France," of whom Shakespeare tells, "as sad as night only for wantonness." Theirs is the same stately and reserved pathos which is depicted on Attic tombstones; the same sadness which penetrates us, when we read in their austere simplicity the last greetings addressed by the tragic heroes to the sunlight and to their homes. The genuine Hellene was touched with a profound pity for the wretchedness of man. Death and fate formed a dark background to his brilliant vision of the universe. Yet there is no trace of weakness or querulous egotism. Without consolation here or hope hereafter he could face his inexorable doom, and by great thoughts and deeds conquer destiny. In the modern world the contradiction between boundless aspiration and limited powers is apt to paralyse high effort. In classical Greek antiquity the sense of man's feebleness heightens his energy of will. The impression left on us is altogether unique in character; and, as a result, the pathetic in Greek poetry is often not far removed from the sublime. "There is nothing, methinks, more piteous than a man, of all things that creep and breathe upon the earth"[1]—these words are uttered by Zeus in the *Iliad*, and the thought is typically Hellenic. But no less Hellenic is the rousing call of Sarpedon to Glaucus: "Ah, friend, if once escaped from this battle we were for ever to be ageless and immortal, neither would I fight myself in the foremost ranks, nor would I send thee into the war that giveth men renown, but now—for assuredly ten thousand fates of death do every way beset us, and these no mortal may escape nor avoid—now let us go forward, whether we shall give glory to other men, or others to us."[2] The dark destiny of man is here the very motive which prompts to heroism. The thought is the same as that of Pindar: "Forasmuch as men must die, wherefore should one sit vainly in the dark through a dull and nameless age, and without lot in noble deeds?"[3]

[1] *Il.* xvii. 446-47.
[2] *Il.* xii. 322-28.
[3] Pind. *Ol.* i. 82-84.

THE WRITTEN AND THE SPOKEN WORD

THE people who of all others have done most for the intellectual progress of the race, whose literature more than once has roused the Western world by the shock of new ideas from lethargy to mental activity, knew but little of books, and looked with some suspicion on writing as of doubtful value for awakening thought. Almost everything, indeed, was to the Greeks worth knowing, but the things most worth knowing they could get best, as they imagined, from the lips of their fellow-men. Of none of them was the remark true which one modern scholar made about another, "that he had read himself into ignorance." In our own day protests have now and then been heard against the mere reading man, the book-worm who values books as such, not so far as they express and interpret to us the truth of life and the thought of men, but with a superstitious reverence for the printed page. Such a protest was tacitly entertained, though not so often expressed, in ancient Greece against the lifeless symbols of writing, the dead letter as opposed to the quickening and responsive energy of oral intercourse, where each sense and faculty—eye and ear and brain—are acting together in busy co-operation and rivalry, each eliciting, stimulating, and supplementing the other.

With us silent reading has superseded many of the social gatherings of friends, and the art of conversation has been falling into disuse. Political speeches from the platform, which, while they fulfil their proper purpose, serve also as a dramatic entertainment and satisfy the combative instincts of mankind, are an influence which, so far from decreasing, gathers fresh force every day. But the influence of speech in other forms is on the decline compared with that of writing. We accept it as a commonplace that in the modern world the invention whose effects have been most far-reaching is the invention of printing. But we sometimes forget that the ancient world made a still greater discovery—the art of writing. The transition from the Spoken to the Written

Word was more startling to the imagination, more revolutionary in its consequences, than the transition from the Written Word to the Printed Page.

Let us for a moment look at the reception which the Greeks, the most keen-witted and original people of antiquity, gave to this great discovery. It was indeed a cold reception, very unlike what might have been expected. Curious as they were to find out and to tell all that their neighbours knew or did, quick to borrow and adapt the ideas of others, they were yet slow to appreciate the full value and significance of this one art. For centuries they employed it, not as a vehicle of thought, but almost wholly for memorial purposes, such as registering treaties and commercial contracts, preserving the names of Olympian victors, fixing boundaries, and the like. Engrossed in poetic legend and mythology, they evinced little desire to transmit the memory of passing events even when these events were of commanding interest. It was the opening of a new era both for historical research and for literature, when Herodotus wrote a history whose inspiring motive was the desire "that neither the deeds of men may fade from memory by lapse of time, nor the mighty and marvellous works wrought partly by Hellenes, partly by Barbarians, may lose their renown."[1] Nor did the early Hellenes trouble themselves with strict chronology. Their historical records were drawn up by the temple-priests, and, in the edifying lessons they contained, bore the impress of their origin. A historic sense was slowly developed. Even after writing had come into general use, the Greeks still thought of it as imported from abroad, and spoke of the alphabet as "Phoenician symbols." They had, in short, no natural turn for learning their letters; and their early inaptitude for reading and writing may be traced down to a late period in their ignorance of foreign alphabets and neglect of foreign literature.

A large measure of the suspicion with which they regarded the written word was, perhaps, due to the manner in which written symbols came to them. The contrast is notable between their case and that of the Egyptians. The signs that the Egyptians employed on their monuments were not mere symbols of sounds, but the images of the

[1] Herod. i. 1, ὡς *μήτε τὰ γενόμενα ἐξ ἀνθρώπων τῷ χρόνῳ ἐξίτηλα γένηται, μήτε ἔργα μεγάλα τε καὶ θαυμαστά, τὰ μὲν Ἕλλησι τὰ δὲ βαρβάροισι ἀποδεχθέντα, ἀκλεᾶ γένηται.*

objects for which they stood. If the Greeks, like the Egyptians, had gone through this process of ideography, writing would, like speaking, have been a sort of art, and therefore held in reverence: it would have been natural, not conventional; and the connexion and even equivalence of the word spoken and the word written would have been manifest. Between words and ideas a necessary connexion was held to exist by one school of Greek thinkers. Names were supposed to be the exact counterpart, vocal imitations, of the things they represented: the correspondence was complete between sound and sense. But though the theory of picture-sounds as an expression of thought was often discussed, it never occurred to the Greeks that writing itself might have come from picture-signs, which were originally an artistic imitation of the objects. They had received from the Phoenicians a set of ready-made symbols, a conventionalised script, whose meaning was not easily discerned, whose use was mechanical, and whose associations were at first almost purely commercial. Written characters were therefore for them stamped from the outset with the mark of utilitarianism, and were as far removed from art as possible.

The severance, however, between writing and the fine arts — beneficent as it was from the artistic point of view, and no less so from the point of view of convenience—was unhappy for the *prestige* of writing, which was long regarded by the Greeks as mechanical, symbolic, almost cabalistic. They dissociated from it the notion of organic beauty and artistic form. Now, as artists they disliked all mere routine, all work that was purely mechanical. The free inspiration of the poet was checked by the use of conventional symbols: the epic and the drama depended, if not for their very existence, at least for their vitality, on the living voice and on listening crowds. Add to this the fact that poetry, with its musical accompaniments, could be carried in the memory without external aids and appliances.

But it was not alone the artistic instinct of the Greeks that made them look with some suspicion upon writing. In conduct, too, they shrank from formulae. Unvarying rules petrified action; the need of flexibility, of perpetual adjustment, was strongly felt. The attitude of the Greek mind towards the laws is a conspicuous case in point.[1]

[1] This idea is brought out in a similar connexion by E. Curtius, *Alterthum und Gegenwart*, i. 254 *sqq*.

Most Eastern nations had religious codes in writing, which were supposed to have come direct from the mind or the hand of God, and were invested with a peculiar sanctity. With the Greeks, however, writing never acquired the consecration of religion. Certain rules of outward and ceremonial worship were preserved in the sanctuaries on inscribed tablets under priestly guardianship; but no system of religious doctrine and observance, no manuals containing authoritative rules of morality, were ever transmitted in documentary form. The laws, which were of divine authorship and origin, whose "life was not of to-day or yesterday," "the day of whose appearing no man knew," were the unwritten laws.

In the domain of secular life and of politics there was a similar reluctance to reduce laws to writing. Great weight was attached to continuous oral traditions, but these traditions were not embodied in formal enactments. The states of Greece proper long remained without written constitutions: these were for the most part framed in the decay of civic life. The earliest written laws of Greece were penal codes; but even in the forensic sphere, the bent of the Greek mind—or at least of Athenian jurymen—was to make light of written technicalities, to think more of what the lawgiver meant than of what the laws said, to make the spirit supreme over the letter. To spiritualise law, however, is a dangerous process. The law is carnal, and law spiritualised is apt to become illegality.

The attempt to infuse into the laws warmth, animation, moral character, and individuality is distinctively Greek. The laws for them are not cold principles once for all embodied in the statute-book. They come forward as living and speaking personalities — questioning, reasoning, appealing, exhorting—and that not only in an imaginative composition, such as the famous passage in the *Crito* of Plato, when the Laws address Socrates in prison, but also in the orators. To Demosthenes the laws of Athens are the permanent and expressive counterpart of Athenian character ; and they can speak to all who know how to question them. Law, as conceived by the Greeks, was not an alien force, a constraint externally imposed, but, like the state itself, part of their being ; the representative of their true, their rational, self, the image of their moral life ; not the denial of individual freedom, but the realisation of freedom.

The sense, then, that the laws represented a personal intelligence probably caused a disinclination to reduce them to written and stereotyped commands. The most ancient Greek traditions concerning the origin of law confirmed this feeling. The inspired decisions (θέμιστες) of the king, as judge, were the foundation of customary law. The earliest law-givers had revelations from the gods in whose confidence they were; Minos was the familiar friend of Zeus, Lycurgus of the Delphic god. When law no longer flowed in inspired words from the lips of the prince, it was still a living voice, the voice of the community, the public reason and conscience expressing itself in articulate form. The laws were in certain states (as in Crete and Sparta) promulgated and conveyed to the people in forms of music and poetry; we read, too, of laws arranged as catches and sung after dinner. The custom of singing the laws is explained by Aristotle[1] as an aid to memory before the invention of writing: we must remember, however, that long after writing was well known in Greece the laws still remained unwritten. That they should have been set to music and associated with festive occasions is fully in accord

[1] Arist. *Probl.* xix. 28.

with the Greek sentiment, which saw in them not stern task-masters, but the companions of social life, friendly and intelligent advisers.

The objection to written laws was presented in this form—that "the endless and irregular movement of human things does not admit of a universal and simple rule": [1] whereas the law aims at a fatal simplicity which neglects individual peculiarities and shifting circumstances. The analogy of medicine was here urged. Written codes were compared to unvarying medical prescriptions.[2] It is a mistake, it was said, to be doctored by formulae. Even in Egypt where a fixed treatment is laid down by law, a doctor may deviate from it after three days if it proves ineffectual. Now, the language of the laws resembles an official medical prescription; it is general and does not meet the particular case. The inference drawn was that the supremacy of the best man is to be preferred to that of the law. Aristotle in noticing the argument rejects the analogy with medicine, and replies that the ruler is liable to self-interested motives from which the physician is free. If the

[1] Plat. *Polit.* 294 B, *αἱ γὰρ ἀνομοιότητες τῶν τε ἀνθρώπων καὶ τῶν πράξεων καὶ τὸ μηδέποτε μηδέν, ὡς ἔπος εἰπεῖν, ἡσυχίαν ἄγειν τῶν ἀνθρωπίνων οὐδὲν ἐῶσιν ἁπλοῦν ἐν οὐδενὶ περὶ ἁπάντων.*

[2] Arist. *Pol.* iii. 15. 1286 a 10 *sqq.* and iii. 16. 1287 a 32 *sqq.*

patient suspected his physician of being bribed to poison him, he would prefer to be doctored by formulae. The written law is indeed a mere formula, but as a formula it has the advantage of being unemotional; law is "reason without impulse."

The need of flexibility felt in conduct was felt no less strongly in the region of philosophy. Truth was a Proteus ever taking new shapes,[1] a manifold and shifting thing, whose secret must be extorted by skill and patience, by the close grappling of dialectic, by the give and take of argument. No written exposition could reproduce the free play and infinite elasticity of thought. The historian Diodorus[2] contrasts unfavourably the restless movement of Greek speculation with the unchanging philosophy transmitted from father to son by the Chaldeans. The Greeks, he says, are always innovating; they do not follow those who have gone before; every day they found new sects; whereas the barbarians hold faithfully to their traditional doctrines. The Greeks of the great period of literature would not have spoken thus. They would not have acquiesced in the praise of philosophic immobility. Plato—except possibly in old age, when he became dogmatic—would have cited

[1] Cp. Plat. *Euthyd.* 288 B. [2] Diodor. Sic. ii. 29.

this as a salient example of the baneful influence of the written word, of those *σήματα λυγρά* which arrest and petrify life.

In him is to be found the most outspoken disparagement of writing, as compared with speech, that occurs in Greek literature. I allude to the passage of the *Phaedrus* where Socrates says that writing is the mere image or phantom of the living and animated word.[1] It does not teach what was not known before; it serves only to remind the reader of something that he already knew.[2] It enfeebles the power of thought. It is delusive even as an aid to memory, for it weakens and supersedes this faculty by providing an artificial substitute. Moreover, it has no power of adaptation; it speaks in one voice to all; it cannot answer questions, meet objections, correct misunderstandings, or supplement its own omissions.

The same idea is repeated and expanded in two of the letters which have come down to us under Plato's name (*Ep.* ii. and vii.). These letters

[1] Plat. *Phaedr.* 276 A, λόγον ζῶντα καὶ ἔμψυχον οὗ ὁ γεγραμμένος εἴδωλον ἄν τι λέγοιτο δικαίως.

[2] On books as a mere record of learning and starting-point of research compare the remarkable sentence of Varro (*Sat. Menipp. Reliq.*): "Libri nonnisi scientiarum paupercula monumenta sunt: principia inquirendorum continent, ut ab his negotiandi principia sumat animus."

profess to be written by Plato to the tyrant Dionysius II., and contain advice as to the proper method of studying philosophy. The view is here enforced that continuous written exposition is useless as a means for arriving at philosophic truth. Some other branches of learning may perhaps be communicated in this way, but not so philosophy. Only by painful effort and self-questioning, by the friction of mind with mind, and by friendly cross-examination, can true knowledge be attained. Thus "by close intercourse with the subject and living familiarity with it, a light is of a sudden kindled in the mind, as from a fire that leaps forth, which when once generated keeps itself alive."[1] Philosophical knowledge breaks in upon the mind as a mental illumination. Such is the metaphor employed, and such the general idea that runs through these letters.

The publication of a systematic treatise on philosophy is here strongly condemned,—Plato's own writings being exempted from this general censure on the ground (by no means a convincing one) that they are purely dramatic compositions

[1] Plat. *Ep.* vii. 341 C, ἐκ πολλῆς συνουσίας γιγνομένης περὶ τὸ πρᾶγμα αὐτὸ καὶ τοῦ συζῆν ἐξαίφνης οἷον ἀπὸ πυρὸς πηδήσαντος ἐξαφθὲν φῶς ἐν τῇ ψυχῇ γενόμενον αὐτὸ ἑαυτὸ ἤδη τρέφει.

and convey no formal doctrine. "It is for this reason," says Plato, or the writer speaking in his name,[1] "that I have never myself written anything upon these subjects. There neither is nor ever shall be a treatise of Plato's. What goes by his name are the words of Socrates." There is, however, in these letters more than the mere dislike of dogmatical exposition. The author's prejudice against publishing a book for the benefit of general readers is expressed in a tone which suggests a feeling of freemasonry in the higher learning. He goes so far as to say[2] that when you see any published writings, either promulgated laws or other compositions, you may be sure that the author, if he was worth anything, did not himself regard these as matters of serious importance: if he did he would not have published them,—unless in a moment of infatuation. The mystery of learning was similarly guarded in the middle ages, and even Bacon inherited the dislike of allowing newly discovered truth to pass beyond an inner circle of disciples.

We have now seen the general line of objection taken by the Greeks to the written and formulated word. An analogy of modern science may serve

[1] Plat. *Ep.* ii. 314 C.

[2] *Ib.* vii. 344 C, D.

further to explain the precise reason of this. One of the most recent definitions of life attempted by the science of biology is "the continuous adjustment of internal relations to external relations" (Herbert Spencer). Death, on the other hand, is "the non-correspondence of the organism with its environment." In a word, vitality is not absolute, but consists in relation; death is the snapping of a connexion, the suspension of a relation. "The most distinctive peculiarity," says Dr. Burdon Sanderson,[1] "of living matter as compared with non-living is that it is ever changing while ever the same; that is, that life is a state of ceaseless change. . . . The word life is used in physiology in what, if you like, may be called a technical sense, and denotes only that state of change with permanence which I have endeavoured to set forth to you."

The Greeks had advanced to no such definition, but they forestalled it by instinct. They felt and expressed it in all that they say of the spoken as opposed to the written word, though they could not enunciate it as a scientific principle. If life be the "continuous adjustment of internal

[1] At the meeting of the British Association as reported in the *Times*, Sept. 13, 1889.

to external relations," that man is most alive who most surely and with the greatest facility adapts himself to an altered environment: that word is most vital which can best transform and transmute itself according to the needs of its surroundings, thereby maintaining with them the most intimate connexion. The written word—so it may be argued—is not self-adjusting and responsive to the changes of its environment; even the spoken word, once formulated, is no less immobile. Both are dead with the first change of external relations. The chain is snapped, the correspondence broken. They have no capacity for "continuous adjustment," no power to enter into new and vital connexions under altered circumstances. Only the living speaker can do this; in him only can truth live; it most lives in him who is most alive. In biological language the best teacher is he who is in most vivid correspondence with his environment—that is, his pupils; who influences them, and in turn is influenced by them. If the environment change, he will most surely readjust himself; he will never suffer that death which is "want of correspondence."

We may push the analogy a little further. The organism may be a fine one, but the faculty of correspondence weak; then the word is partially dead. The man is richly stored with wisdom, but it is devitalised, because uncommunicated. Or the environment may be poor, but the organism and the faculty of correspondence, fine. Only when all these factors are of high excellence—organism, environment, correspondence—is the word entirely vital.

It is easy to see how this truth would be instinctive in the Greek mind. They were a people highly gifted as individuals, keenly sociable as a community; they were therefore not likely to leave out of their conception of the living word the notion of correspondence, of continuous adjustment. Indeed this is precisely the point on which Plato lays stress in the well-known passage of the *Phaedrus*. "There is one inconvenience in written speech, which is in fact incident to painting also. The creations of the painter have the attitude of life, and yet if you ask them a question they preserve a solemn silence. And the same may be said of written speeches. You might fancy that they had some intelligence of the meaning of what they say, but if you want to know anything and put a question to one of them, they give the same unvarying answer. And when they have been once written down they are tossed about anywhere among those who do and among those who do not understand them. And they have no reticences or proprieties towards different classes of persons; and if they are unjustly assailed or abused, their parent is needed to defend his offspring, for they cannot protect or defend themselves."[1] This dead letter is contrasted with the word of knowledge—the "intelligent writing which is graven in the soul of him who has learned, and can defend itself, and knows when to speak and when to be silent."[2]

No doubt—partly owing to the early prejudice against written mechanical symbols—they added to the notion of the living word some thought of its organic beauty. They suspected in the written language of plain prose an indifference to form, a dulness, an ugliness which was in their minds associated with death, and hence with sterility. Beauty alone (as with Plato) was fecund and creative. Here, perhaps, is one consideration which may partially explain why it was that the Greeks bestowed such minute and unsparing labour on their written compositions—why Plato, the depreciator of literature, was not satisfied till

[1] Plat. *Phaedr.* 275 D. [2] *Ib.* 276 A.

he had written out the first eight words of the *Republic* (as was said to have been discovered after his death) in several different orders; why Demosthenes, whose face was set towards action, wrote and rewrote his speeches, would not trust to premeditation, neglected no detail of language or rhythm. Prose, it was felt, in order to be vital, must have the coherence, the perfection, of a living organism. A newly found art, it must employ every resource which could secure its permanence. Dionysius of Halicarnassus observes that Herodotus was the first who showed that prose could rival the highest poetry in persuasive power, in charm of expression and a capacity of exquisite delight.[1] In itself prose had a low vitality. Its existence was precarious. It was not like poetry, which was wedded to musical strains and lived on the lips of men. Raised as it had been out of the sphere of the inorganic, and resting on lifeless symbols, it might fall back into extinction. It must be clothed upon with beauty, it must learn a music of its own, and so become imperishable.

All spoken words, however, are not vital any

[1] Dionys. Halic. *de Thucyd.* ch. 23, p. 865, *παρεσκεύασε τῇ κρατίστῃ ποιήσει τὴν πέζην φράσιν ὁμοίαν γενέσθαι, πειθοῦς τε καὶ χαρίτων καὶ τῆς εἰς ἄκρον ἡκούσης ἡδονῆς ἕνεκα.*

more than all written words are dead. This did not escape the observation of the Greeks. One test of life is the capacity to impart life. No speech is vital which does not engender thought in those to whom it is addressed. Is it not a distinguishing feature of the highest eloquence that it stimulates and promotes reflection? it is not content with gratifying the ear, with eliciting applause, with ministering to the vanity of the speaker or the prejudices and passions of the audience. It awakens the reasoning faculty, it stirs it into active and sympathetic movement; it has in it the virtue of a creative act; in a word, it sets men thinking. We remember the keynote of the appeals of Demosthenes: "In God's name, I beg of you to think." The spoken word does not always set men thinking. The object of some speeches—of many political speeches—is to prevent men from thinking, to administer a narcotic to the reason. The living voice can be at least as lifeless as the written page. Without the interchange of dialogue—whether oral conversation, or the dialogue that the listener's mind holds with itself, that is, the inward reflection which is kindled by the breath of genuine eloquence—without this, a spoken speech may be as much devitalised as the same speech when committed to paper. One is, in fact, the mere transcript of the other. There is a passage[1] in which Plato describes the harangues, the set speeches of the public men of his day. They are as bad, he says, as books. They go on interminably, but they promote no interchange of thought; they neither ask nor answer questions; they are like brazen pots or pans, which, when once struck, continue to resound till a hand is placed upon them.

Plato had a clear apprehension of what was vital in spoken speech. But he does not appear to have seen in how true a sense a book may be said to be alive. To return to our illustration: the life of a great work of literature consists precisely in its faculty of "continuous adjustment" to a changing environment. *Plus ça change plus c'est la même chose.* There are books, poems in particular, whose vitality is inexhaustible, which have fresh meanings for every age. "The author," we are sometimes reminded, "was not conscious of all these meanings; your interpretation of him is fanciful; you are reading into him the ideas of other times; you find in him more than was

[1] Plat. *Protag.* 329 A.

intended." Yes, but this is the very evidence that the book has life, that it is a living organism of a high and complex character, mobile and sensitive to its surroundings. It has latent correspondences with human nature, which time alone discovers; it has the spontaneous activity, the unconscious self-adapting power of genius. The greater the genius of the writer the more responsive will the book be to its environment, the greater will be the area over which its relations extend, the more far-reaching, both in time and space, the range of its correspondences. For genius is, in fact, life and the faculty of engendering life in others. "A good book," says Milton, "is the precious life-blood of a master-spirit embalmed and treasured up on purpose to a life beyond life"; or, as Bacon puts it, "neither are they (books) fitly to be called images, because they generate still, and cast their seeds in the minds of others, provoking and causing infinite actions and opinions in succeeding ages."

Yet when we speak of life, whether actual, or, as in literature and art, metaphorical, we must remember that it is always a mystery. We can analyse its results, we can declare its conditions, we can never seize its essence. As in genius itself there is something of the wind that bloweth where it listeth, so in the productions of genius the secret of their vitality still eludes us. But we feel that the vitality is there and can test it by the life which it communicates to others. Some literature possesses this life-giving virtue in a surpassing degree. "One of the arguments," says Lowell, "against the compulsory study of Greek, namely, that it is wise to give our time to modern languages and ancient history, involves, I think, a verbal fallacy. Only those languages can properly be called dead in which nothing living has been written. If the classic languages are dead, they yet speak to us, and with a clearer voice than that of any living tongue. If their language is dead, yet the literature it enshrines is rammed with life as perhaps no other writing, except Shakespeare's, ever was or will be. It is as contemporary with to-day as with the ears it first enraptured, for it appeals not to the man of then or now, but to the entire round of human nature itself. . . . We know not whither other studies will lead us, especially if dissociated from this; we do know to what summits, far above our lower region of turmoil, this has led, and what the many-sided outlook thence."

What we have been saying is applicable in a

unique sense to the Bible, which, as a vital growth, has nourished the spiritual life of successive generations, and has seen the death of creeds and sects, the crumbling away of systems of theology which are mere abstracts and digests of truth, not the living food. It is the one book which appears to have the capacity of eternal self-adjustment, of uninterrupted correspondence with an ever shifting and ever widening environment.

Another reason for Plato's distrust of books—in addition to their incapacity for continuous adjustment—attaches itself to the high conception he had formed of the dignity of knowledge. True knowledge is not among marketable wares, that can be dealt in retail or wholesale at the pleasure of the consumer, that can be provided ready-made, carried about in a portable shape in books, and emptied from them into the mind of the learner, as from vessel to vessel. The tendency of language is to describe knowledge in terms of property, as so much wealth acquired or transmitted. But, as the Greeks felt, true knowledge is not an extrinsic advantage, but a hard-won possession, personal and inalienable; it is an inheritance which we must earn in order to possess it. We can enter on it only when we make it our own. It is not mere acquisition, but mental enlargement, inward illumination. Knowledge, as a mere bundle of facts, is not power. Knowledge becomes Power only when it is vitalised by Reason.

"Much learning does not teach wisdom," [1] was a saying of Heraclitus; and Aristotle, whose house was known as "the house of the reader," declared that "much learning produces much confusion." [2] This is not the sigh of intellectual disillusion which we overhear in the words of the author of the book of Ecclesiastes, "He that increaseth knowledge increaseth sorrow," "Much study is a weariness of the flesh." It is the demand for a science which will enable us to organise what we learn. A multifarious learning, for which the Greeks had a single distinctive word, does not imply any connected view of knowledge as a whole, or of the relation in which any one branch of learning stands to other departments. A mass of facts held in the memory may still remain unpenetrated by the light of reason. The subject-matter of knowledge must not be passively received, but sub-

[1] *πολυμαθίη νόον οὐ διδάσκει.* Cp. Plat. *Laws* vii. 811 B, *κίνδυνόν φημι εἶναι φέρουσαν τοῖς παισὶ τὴν πολυμαθίαν*: and 819 A, *ἡ πολυπειρία καὶ πολυμαθία κ.τ.λ.*

[2] Arist. Fr. 51. 1484 a 39, *πολυμάθεια πολλὰς ταραχὰς ποιεῖ.*

mitted to the action of a formative mind, which works upon the impressions, invests them with a meaning, adjusts their relations, reduces them to order and coherence. Then only does knowledge become luminous and philosophic.

The Greeks in their desire to find uniformity in nature and a rational meaning in history, imposed their own thought upon the universe, and anticipated the slow results of science. Yet it was well for the world that they had this passionate trust in the power of reason: it would have been a calamity if, baffled in their first ardour for knowledge, they had become "misologists"—to use Plato's term [1]—or haters of reason, as others become misanthropists or haters of mankind, when they have been deceived in those whom they have trusted. As it was, they conceived the exercise of Logos as Rational Thought to be inseparable from the use of Logos as Rational Speech. The action of a formative mind upon the material of knowledge could hardly, they thought, fully operate without the collision of two personal intelligences, without the play of mind upon mind, the interchange of question and answer, the colloquial commerce of thought. One great charm of Greek

[1] Plat. *Phaedo* 89 D.

literature is, that in reading it we seem to be present at the first awakening of the universal human reason; we seem to watch and overhear it as it becomes conscious of itself. It does not yet speak quite like a book. It is thinking aloud. It debates with itself as with an antagonist; as soon as it becomes articulate it puts the dialectical process before us in vivid and dramatic form. Philosophy shapes itself into a dramatic conversation. History is not a chronicle or bare narrative of events: a running comment of speech accompanies action, as the chorus does the action of the drama; the actors themselves discuss and explain their own motives; thought passes into words which interpret the inner conflicts and make the deeds intelligible.

Now, the Greeks were talkers, whereas we are readers. We read, or else we gossip—both very good things in their way, but they are not all. Speech and writing admit of other combinations than this; and in a University, if anywhere, ought to be the meeting-point and place of reconciliation of these two factors of our intellectual life. Books we have, of course; and speech too there is, or ought to be, in every one of its many forms. We have oral teaching, for example. Some tell us that a University which teaches is an anachronism and a survival; that Universities of this type came into existence at a time when learning could only be had through teachers, but that the invention of printing has superseded oral instruction, and transformed the idea of a University; that the true University is now a library; and the old Universities, if they continue to exist, should exist only for the discovery of truth, not for the diffusion of knowledge—for research, not for education.

This might be a tempting view to hold if it were not for certain facts of our experience. Most of us have observed, and often with much surprise, the mysterious virtue that resides in the living voice of the teacher—or shall we call it a strange weakness in the mind of the student?—which causes a lecture of very moderate merit (provided it is clear and fairly well arranged) to arrest the attention of the listener, when the same thing, expressed in a more finished and complete form, if read in a book awakens the most languid interest. This often happens even where the lecturer has no remarkable personality, and no special attractions of voice and manner. The reason, perhaps, is partly to be found in this—that the speaker is human. That is a fact of ceaseless interest to his fellow-creatures. Most books are in a sense unhuman. How few men write like themselves and give us a true impression of what they are! Once on paper, men are apt to lose their own character, and either to become neutral and impersonal, or to take—unconsciously—a fictitious personality. When we meet the writer afterwards we are tantalised, almost angry with him, for having led us astray. Now, the speaker, or at least the teacher, cannot long wear a mask. He cannot keep up the neutrality of a book. You get to know him at the same time that you learn the subject he is talking about. To come into contact with learning in a human and embodied form has a peculiar mental stimulus of its own.

I do not propose to enter here upon any formal defence of oral instruction. It will be enough to quote some words of Newman's,[1] which sum up admirably most of what can be said upon this topic :—

"If the actions of men may be taken as any test of their conviction, then we have reason for saying this, viz., that the province and the inestimable benefit of the *littera scripta* is that of

[1] *Historical Sketches*, i. 8, 9.

being a record of truth, and an authority of appeal, and an instrument of teaching in the hands of a teacher; but that, if we wish to become exact and fully furnished in any branch of knowledge which is diversified and complicated, we must consult the living man and listen to his living voice. I am not bound to investigate the cause of this, and anything I may say will, I am conscious, be short of its full analysis;—perhaps we may suggest that no books can get through the number of minute questions which it is possible to ask on any extended subject, or can hit upon the very difficulties which are severally felt by each reader in succession. Or, again, that no book can convey the special spirit and delicate peculiarities of its subject with that rapidity and certainty which attend on the sympathy of mind with mind, through the eyes, the look, the accent and the manner, in casual expressions thrown off at the moment, and the unstudied turns of familiar conversation.

" Whatever be the cause the fact is undeniable. The general principles of any study you may learn by books at home; but the detail, the colour, the tone, the air, the life which makes it live in us, you must catch all those from those in whom it lives already. You must imitate the student in French or German, who is not content with his grammar, but goes to Paris or Dresden: you must take example from the young artist who aspires to visit the great masters in Florence and in Rome. Till we have discovered some intellectual daguerreotype which takes off the course of thought, and the form, lineaments, and features of truth as completely and minutely as the optical instrument reproduces the sensible object, we must come to the teachers of wisdom to learn wisdom, we must repair to the fountain, and drink there. Portions of it may go from thence to the ends of the earth by means of books; but the fulness is in one place alone. It is in such assemblages and congregations of intellect that books themselves, the masterpieces of human genius, are written, or at least originated."

In its literary aspect the union of the two principles we have been considering—the Spoken and the Written Word—is vital to the well-being of each. In some nations the literary language is out of all relation to the spoken. In China writing has existed from time immemorial, but chiefly as an official art, a means of government, not an expression of the mind and thought of the people. Even in Latin the spoken and the written language stood far apart, and the breach continued to widen till classical Latin lost the vitality necessary to make it a medium of conversation. In modern Italy literature has by custom come to be written in a single dialect, the Tuscan. A true national literature seldom exists under such conditions. Greek writers on the other hand combined the popular and the literary idiom with a felicity to which there is no parallel except perhaps in English literature. The Greek language had reached maturity before it came under the influence of writing; and the literature retained the freshness, the directness, the simplicity of the best speaking—that charm which so quickly vanishes when style comes to be an art cultivated for its own sake. In the classical age there was no severance between literature and life; writers and thinkers were citizens and men of action. Later, they lost touch of popular sentiment, and literature was sensitive to the change. The divorce between speech and writing led to pedantry, bookishness, and unreality.

It is for the interest of thought as well as of literature to combine the habit of speech with that of writing. Some of us are perhaps inclined to become mere absorbers of books, or possessors of note-books ;—I say "possessors," for one knows of men whose thinking is all in their note-books, not in their heads, there put by for future use against a day that probably never comes ; knowledge not in hand but in store. Speech is indeed the indispensable supplement to reading and writing ; we are aware how often conversation clears the mind, and dispels difficulties which on paper seemed insoluble : nor can this old, this rival method of oral discussion ever be superseded. Some of us look back in after-life to evenings spent in college—in which we talked things out up to late hours of the night, till our brains glowed with excitement and sleep became almost impossible—as among the keenest enjoyments we have ever known. It is one of the distinctive merits of a University that study and social intercourse here go hand in hand ; men and books are being learnt together. At the moment when the powers of the mind are ripening and expanding under the influence of systematic learning, we are taking also our first lessons in life and character. Knowledge is humanised ; it is brought home to us through the affections and the imagination as well as through the reason ; we and it are more nearly identified ; it is enriched and elevated by the associations of friendship, by the joy of free and fearless discussion among equals, by ennobling rivalries, and by still more ennobling intellectual partnerships. In the meeting and collision of mind and mind, in the ready sympathy of friends, in the quick movements of kindred intelligences which outstrip and correct and interpret one another's reasonings, we have thought produced on principles that are unknown to workshops and factories. It is more like creation than production. The original material is found to have grown and multiplied. Knowledge thus humanised is already half-way to Wisdom ; for Knowledge becomes Wisdom only when it has been brought into contact with life.

THE UNITY OF LEARNING

IN the *Vicar of Wakefield* the Principal of the University of Louvain makes the following observations :—"You see me, young man, I never learned Greek, and don't find that I have ever missed it. I have had a doctor's cap and gown without Greek; I have 10,000 florins a year without Greek; I eat heartily without Greek; and in short," continued he, "as I don't know Greek, I do not believe there is any good in it." We will not now discuss whether any one ever got any good out of Greek. But the words I have just quoted undoubtedly express the attitude of mind with which University training is still pretty widely regarded.

If we were to ask the average citizen who had never happened to pay special attention to the subject, what was taught in Colleges and Universities, he would probably answer, *useless learning*. And it is perhaps not such a bad answer after all; in a certain sense we may even make it our own, and claim it as a distinction that, in the seats of Academic learning, little or nothing "useful" is taught. Their aim is not to turn out doctors, clergy, lawyers, merchants, but men—and now women also—with thoroughly trained minds, minds fortified and enlarged by various disciplines, and fitted not for this or that profession but for the conduct of life. To teach people how to think is perhaps the highest end of education, and to learn to think the most difficult thing a man is ever called on to do. A democratic society is inclined to do its thinking by deputy, if only it is permitted to do its voting individually. It is so easy to think in herds through Committees and sub-Committees and party organisations. To exercise the thinking power for its own sake is the central idea of Academic studies. Suppress thinking and you will be able to suppress freedom itself.

Voltaire, in a paper on the "Horrible Danger of Reading," imagines an edict of the Sublime Porte condemning, proscribing, anathematising the infernal invention of printing for reasons which are then enumerated. "For these and other causes," the edict proceeds, "for the edification of the faithful and for the good of their souls we forbid them ever to read a book under pain of eternal damnation. . . . And to prevent any infringement of our ordinance we expressly forbid them *to think* under the same penalties; and we enjoin on all true believers the duty of informing us of any one who shall have pronounced four connected phrases, from which any clear and distinct sense can be extracted. We therefore ordain that in all conversation terms must be used that signify nothing according to the ancient usage of the Sublime Porte. Given in our Palace of Stupidity, etc."

The growth of Academic learning and the foundation of new Colleges in this country is plain proof that the younger generation has refused to take the Vow of Ignorance. Here we have their public confession that they are not content with intellectual livelihood, they ask for intellectual life. What is desired is to broaden the basis of our education, to make it truly liberal, in the sense that it shall emancipate the mind from what is narrow, local, partial. Not learning only is to be acquired, but, if possible, also that wisdom which is the last result of mature knowledge. The wish to get on in the world, to win success, is doubtless present, but the success to be aimed at is of a durable kind. It is not to be achieved by the cast of a die or by a lucky hit. A fortune, as it is understood in the mercantile world, may sometimes be made by a stroke of business ; on the other hand it may be lost as quickly as it was gained. The fortune which belongs to the things of the mind is outside the region of luck. It is not a speculation, it is a fortune slowly built up ; every step is won by toil ; but once ours it is ours for ever. We may increase our intellectual wealth by labour, but we cannot lose it except by repeated acts of wilful surrender. It may or may not bring financial success : it is pretty certain not to make millionaires : but it is a possession which those who have acquired will not exchange for any lower kind of wealth.

In its original and proper function a University is a place for the training of the human mind as such, without reference to the special vocations of after-life. The motive, the governing principle, is the disinterested love of knowledge—knowledge, not as a means to an end but as in itself a good. Literature, Art, and Science—

these are the three chief disciplines by which man seeks to attain truth or strives after beauty; and these departments are so inherently connected together as to form an ideal unity. They are the nucleus of University learning, they embody the idea that underlies a University; nor is it any disparagement to the other studies to say that we have here the core and heart of the system, the common source from which professional studies and faculties derive their theoretic principles, and apart from which they cannot attain their specific ends.

The Sciences of Medicine, Law, and Theology—practical sciences as they may be called,—do not aim at scientific knowledge as such, though scientific knowledge is a condition of their success. To pursue knowledge for its own sake and apart from practical applications is strictly speaking the purpose and idea of a University discipline in Arts and Science. What is in some Universities of our country known as the Faculty of Arts, and in Germany as the Philosophical Faculty, in which language, philosophy, literature, and the pure sciences—mathematical, physical, and natural sciences—all meet, is the connecting link which unites

Academical learning with professional study. It reaches out into border territories and everywhere finds common ground. So long as the idea on which it rests is operative a University cannot become a mere group of departmental schools, or a polytechnic institute. The historical and the philosophical group of subjects stands in close relation to the Faculties of Law and of Theology; they supply, or ought to supply, the theoretic basis on which the latter rest; while the department of Mathematics, in its intimate union with the physical and to some extent with the natural sciences, allies itself with Medicine.

The Arts and Sciences, then, as taught in a University are the pledge of the Unity of Learning,—that old Greek idea embodied in the word Philosophy, which is in danger of being lost in the growing specialism of our age. Socrates in the *Phaedo*[1] speaks of his delight at the first utterance of the word "Mind." He who uttered it, says Aristotle,[2] stood out as a sober man among random talkers." It must be owned that the Greeks were sometimes carried away by this

[1] Plat. *Phaed.* 97 C.

[2] Arist. *Met.* i. 3. 984 b 17, οἷον νήφων ἐφάνη παρ' εἰκῇ λέγοντας τοὺς πρότερον.

discovery. They were misled by their own intellectual ardour, by their indomitable impulse to know. They saw that there must be an intelligible law of things, and impatiently they anticipated it. They could not always wait to read the "long and difficult language of facts."[1] Their unifying instinct tyrannised over them. Not only was this so in natural science and in the philosophy of mind; their early historical records and popular traditions also suffer from a premature attempt to make the course of events rational, to import order and symmetry into history, to trace the action and method of divine government without a sufficient basis of facts.

Yet for all this it was a fruitful and inspiring passion—this belief in a constructive reason, in an order of things which the human mind can discover, in a Philosophy that was "the knowledge of all things human and divine." In the course of centuries the authority of such a Philosophy has been challenged; it has been divested of its prerogatives; its functions have been parcelled out among specialised sciences; its separate departments have become independent branches of

[1] Plat. *Polit.* 278 D, *τὰς τῶν πραγμάτων μακρὰς καὶ μὴ ῥᾳδίους συλλαβάς.*

knowledge, each following its own method and obeying laws of its own. Philosophy, as many would contend, has been dethroned, and is no longer the Science among the Sciences; some would deny that it has any scientific claims whatever. Philosophy, it is said, must be content with the dream-land of the Absolute: it may amuse itself with solving the insoluble problems.

Now it may be observed that the principle of specialisation which is supposed to have dethroned Philosophy, not only rules, as it ought in some sense to rule, in the intellectual and industrial domains, but is beginning also to claim sway over the life of the individual. I have heard of an organisation which pledges its members to read a solid book for one half-hour a day. Whether the half-hour may be taken in separate doses of so many minutes each, I do not know. But at any rate the half-hour's reading must be got through under penalty of paying a fine; and it is said that as midnight draws near there is sometimes in festive gatherings a flutter and a stir among those who have barely left themselves time to retrieve the day. As this is a highly specialised association for the promotion of culture, so there are other similar associations for the supervision of morals. Every part of a man's nature has a Vigilance Committee or Society appointed to superintend it. Morality is divided into its component elements; in Plato's phrase, Virtue is "broken up into small change."[1] The danger of such piecemeal morality is a very real one,—that these several departments each impressed with its own primary importance may aspire to constitute the whole of virtue, or may even set up separate and unauthorised codes of their own. Now if such external props and aids to virtue are needed, if departmental supervision must be exercised over morality in its various aspects, at least let it be borne in mind that there still exists a connected scheme of virtues and duties, a law of right conduct that is supreme over all forms and phases of individual life; that there are many virtues, yet that Virtue is one; that though there are ten commandments in the decalogue, there is still one Righteousness.

We cannot indeed wonder that specialisation should sometimes be pushed beyond its proper limits when we see the vast fields of knowledge that have been opened up by this method. Yet it is none the less true that excessive specialisa-

[1] Plat. *Meno* 79 A, κερματίζειν τὴν ἀρετήν.

tion is the death of Science. It is so even in the case of a single science. In ancient Egypt, we are told, there was a special class of physicians for each part of the human body and for each kind of illness. None of these doctors treated the body as a whole. Scientific medicine was therefore impossible. Excessive specialisation would moreover ultimately involve the dissolution of society. Conceive, if you can, a world of specialists, in which each man's vision and labour are concentrated on some microscopic point in the field of human activity, and the very idea of a political and social organism disappears. There is a point at which the subdivision of labour in the intellectual sphere must be checked, and some unifying principle introduced, if we are to retain any rational conception of man, or of the world, or of human life.

The commonwealth of learning is at present endangered by disintegrating tendencies. A single science in the course of a few years is multiplied into half a dozen sciences: mere *disiecta membra* of knowledge they will be unless they are reunited by constructive thought and held together by some regulative and master principle. Here, then, comes in the function of

Philosophy—to survey the whole field of labour even to its farthest limits ; to exhibit the common principles underlying the several sciences, the laws of thought which govern their methods ; to harmonise their results and reduce to unity their highest generalisations : in a word, to bind together the many domains and outlying provinces of learning and to form them into a system. Plato formed a grand idea of Philosophy, as that comprehensive science which embraces not only logic and ethics and metaphysics, but also the study of politics, of religion, of fine art, of social science, of language, and of education. It was an idea impossible to realise in the infancy of the sciences, but it was a vision from the mount of prophecy ; it is still a vision, but a waking vision, and no mere dream. Philosophy may hope to be restored to something like her old supremacy through the agency of those very sciences which have dethroned her. Their highest generalisations are for her the points of departure ; they are the materials on which she works. Philosophy should aspire to become the Science of the Sciences, the unity and meeting-point of all, including all and yet distinct from each.

It is precisely this ideal Unity of the Sciences that is represented by a University as a place of learning and research. Not that every student must necessarily be trained in technical philosophy; still all ought to be initiated into the principles of knowledge, taught not only how to know this or that, but how to *know*. All should acquire a certain habit of mind, an enlargement of view and breadth of judgment. This expansion of the mind is what we need in the professions as well as in the pursuits of liberal learning. The saying of Galen, *ἄριστος ἰατρὸς καὶ φιλόσοφος*, "the best physician is also a philosopher"—a man of philosophic mind—is still true, though medicine has become one of the most specialised of the sciences. In a similar spirit Aristotle[1] distinguishes the technical knowledge of a science from the knowledge of scientific method. A man of general philosophic culture will, he says, be able to form a competent judgment on the specialist's treatment of his own branch of study. Such a critical faculty, which

[1] Arist. *de Part. Anim.* i. 1. 639 a 1-10: it is the mark of *τὸν ὅλως πεπαιδευμένον* to be able *κρῖναι εὐστόχως τί καλῶς ἢ μὴ ἀποδίδωσιν ὁ λέγων*. He may be regarded as *περὶ πάντων ὡς εἰπεῖν κριτικόν τινα*. Similarly *Met.* α 3. 995 a 12-14 the knowledge of an *ἐπιστήμη* and of the *τρόπος* ("method") *ἐπιστήμης* are distinguished.

can be applied to almost any subject, he looks on as the highest and most characteristic result of a liberal education.

Though the methods of the sciences may differ, the method of learning is one; and in all education the method is at least as important as the instruction conveyed. Every people that has set a value upon the things of the mind has recognised this fact. Socrates pressed it home upon his own generation. Vital knowledge cannot, like common wares, be passed from hand to hand: it cannot be mechanically conveyed into the mind as so much mental furniture. "How I wish," said Socrates, in the *Symposium*,[1] as he took his seat by his friend the poet Agathon, "that wisdom could be infused through the medium of touch, out of the full into the empty man, like the water which the wool sucks out of the full vessel into an empty one; in that case how much I should prize sitting by you!" But Socrates knew that this was just what could not be. No teacher that ever lived has shown with such compelling force as Socrates himself

[1] Plat. *Symp.* 175 D (Jowett's Trans.), εὖ ἂν ἔχοι, φάναι, ὦ Ἀγάθων, εἰ τοιοῦτον εἴη ἡ σοφία, ὥστ' ἐκ τοῦ πληρεστέρου εἰς τὸν κενώτερον ῥεῖν ἡμῶν, ἐὰν ἁπτώμεθα ἀλλήλων, ὥσπερ τὸ ἐν ταῖς κύλιξιν ὕδωρ τὸ διὰ τοῦ ἐρίου ῥέον ἐκ τῆς πληρεστέρας εἰς τὴν κενωτέραν. εἰ γὰρ οὕτως ἔχει καὶ ἡ σοφία, πολλοῦ τιμῶμαι τὴν παρὰ σοὶ κατάκλισιν.

how unlike learning is to mechanical acquisition. One reason for his bitter hostility to the methods and pretensions of the Sophists was that they encouraged, as he believed, the delusion that mental culture may be externally received and acquired,[1] that ready-made intellectual results can be supplied, if only the market value of the commodity is fixed.

Aristotle,[2] too, speaks of the "rapid but unscientific" method of the teaching of the Sophists. They fancied they were imparting education when they were only imparting results (*οὐ γὰρ τέχνην ἀλλὰ τὰ ἀπὸ τῆς τέχνης διδόντες παιδεύειν ὑπελάμβανον*): and he illustrates their method by the example of a shoemaker, who, professing to teach the art of making painless shoes, put into the apprentice's hand a large assortment of shoes ready-made (*δοίη δὲ πολλὰ γένη παντοδαπῶν ὑποδημάτων*). There are no tricky short cuts to knowledge. "Learning," Aristotle elsewhere says, "is painful,"[3] and teaching too is difficult. To evoke the thinking process in another, to guide

[1] Cp. Plat. *Rep.* 518 C, φασὶ δέ που οὐκ ἐνούσης ἐν τῇ ψυχῇ ἐπιστήμης σφεῖς ἐντιθέναι, where the word ἐντιθέναι suggests what we call the "cram" system. See also *Protag.* 314 A-B.

[2] Arist. *Soph. Elench.* 33. 184 a 2-8.

[3] Arist. *Pol.* v. (viii.) 1339 a 28, μετὰ λύπης γὰρ ἡ μάθησις.

the mind without forcing it, to follow and understand a pupil's thought even when it is misdirected—this is, in its highest perfection, the gift of a Socrates and of a few born teachers, yet it is also the ideal at which all teachers ought to aim.

If we would gain any orderly conception of knowledge as a whole, we should each begin by seeking after unity in his own department. Some one or two branches of study within our department are probably more familiar to us than the others; they form a solid tract of land which we have reclaimed from the waste and made our own. But we ought to know enough of all branches of our subject to think out their connexions, and to bring them into organic relation with one another. We shall then be the better prepared to pass on to the other sciences where different methods and new intellectual processes are involved, and to fit them into the general system of our thought. The guidance of a good teacher here becomes a matter of the first moment to the pupil.

The same subject may be taught, the same book read, the same information given, but the whole difference to the pupil is in the way it is done. It is not the result that is of value, but how you get the result. The method it is that makes the teacher. A man of large and liberal culture will treat even the rudiments of his subject differently from one who has, so to speak, just learnt his own lesson, or has an eye only to the coming examination. The true teacher cannot forget that his subject is a unity. He will not neglect the whole in the part. At each stage of progress he will give glimpses into something beyond. Beginning with particulars, he will in and through them lead up to principles. He will interpret the details, and make them orderly and intelligible by the illuminating force of reason. At the same time he will be aware that his own department is related to a larger whole, to that which constitutes the unity of knowledge itself. He will not deal with his subject in the narrow spirit of one who has acquired some technical aptitude and seeks to make his own craft usurp the whole universe. The craftsman looks to one thing only; he has not the time or training to see the relations in which his own special subject stands to other pursuits. It is enough for him if he can make that one field of human activity his own, though it may be infinitesimally small.

Now the teacher and the student should imitate the craftsman in thoroughness, minuteness, and precision. He must not be led away by the charlatan's view that thoroughness means pedantry. Pedantry is not accuracy, precision of thought, mastery of detail. It means disproportion and loss of perspective; a lingering over minutiae till all the sense of the whole is lost. It means the learning which cannot organise what we know even in a single department, much less take a survey of any wider field. The pedant becomes a slave to rules which are made by the abstract understanding, working within too limited a sphere and divorced from real insight. Pedantry is rigid and lifeless not so much because it draws too fine distinctions; rather, the pedant's distinctions are not fine enough, he does not allow for the variety which is to be found in the concrete world; he seeks to bring the contents of his thought under the bondage of the letter. The living truths of nature, art, literature escape the apprehension of one who moves in the atmosphere of intellectual abstraction. Not less but greater grasp of detail is needed; of a kind, however, which implies wider horizons, an enlargement of the whole mental outlook. It is the distinctive mark of a University education to give a thoroughness which is not pedantry, and an enlargement of mind which does not lose itself in generalities.

Such an attitude and quality of mind is not, of course, the exclusive gift of University training. It is not the privilege of the few, an aristocratic freemasonry from which common men are shut out. It is found in some who have but little book knowledge, and who have got their chief learning from life—in the market-place, in the counting-house, in the workshop, and in the camp. Still, whatever failures have to be recorded against University education, it is the distinctive aim and office of a University, as the home of the undivided sciences, to bestow this grasp of mind, this sureness of insight, this comprehensive judgment. And if it is of supreme importance to a community to keep its men of intellect in touch with the people and with their mental life, it devolves on all who are trained in Academic learning to do their utmost to foster that philosophic breadth and largeness of view which rests on moral no less than on intellectual sympathy.

Excessive specialism tends to divorce Learning from Life; the men of Thought from the men of

Action; the Scholar from the Citizen; to place a great gulf between the world of the Learned and the world of the Unlearned. That gulf it is the duty of men of learning to bridge over. Those who have the clearest consciousness of the unity of knowledge ought also most vividly to realise the unity of civic life; for the human reason which lays down the regulative principles of thought is one and the same as that reason which has worked in history, imposing its dictates upon men and upon nations, directing their blind instincts and moulding their institutions. The same force of reason which is at the basis of science is at the basis also of society. It is the principle of unity which knits us together into an intellectual and civic community. Thought and action, knowing and doing, are not opposing and conflicting principles. Their harmony and equilibrium are essential to the sanity of a people. Where the balance and due correspondence between the principles are lost, a nation runs into fanaticism or sinks into sloth.

No one will deny that there are in every generation and in every people some solitary thinkers, who best fulfil the purpose of their life by standing aloof from the activities of ordinary men, devoting themselves in the study or the laboratory to that wherein the bent of their genius lies. All action does not consist in external acts; there are men whose *knowing* is their *doing*, and whose inward and silent energy may work upon the world at large with a force greater than that of conquerors or of statesmen. Nor would we suggest that the less distinguished men, whose path still lies in the field of intellect—in literature or science or education—must of necessity become party politicians if they are to do their duty as citizens. It is surely no great harm that there should be a few who are detached from the service of party, especially if they are able thereby to take a clearer and larger outlook over politics and to see beyond the party triumphs of the hour.

Still the learned world has not, perhaps, always been mindful of what is due from it to the society of which it forms a part. It has too often fancied itself to be in possession of some enchanted ground, and to hold the key to mysteries which none else may open. The very dialect of learning has often been enough to frighten off intruders. You required a special noviciate to understand it. In order to be profound it was thought necessary to be obscure. Learned exposition must needs be unintelligible to men of culture who had not acquired the formulae and mannerisms of the craft. Learned men, we may hope, are ceasing to think of themselves as a guild or exclusive fraternity. The great scientific discoverers of our age—a Darwin and a Pasteur—are models of good writing. They are bent on saying what they mean and on saying it clearly—the first secret of style—and the words are exactly adequate to the thought that is to be expressed. Even the philosophers who have long been the worst offenders are following the example of the leaders of science and learning to write with a view to be understood. Nothing is so hard but that it can be said clearly as well as obscurely. What is intrinsically hard cannot, of course, be made easy; but it is capable of being made clear to a trained intelligence.

This single fact, that learned men are acquiring the use of their mother tongue, is already producing a remarkable influence on the diffusion of knowledge, and doing much to efface the sharp distinction between the learned and the unlearned. The distinction can, indeed, never be completely effaced. There are whole departments of knowledge whose processes can only be followed by a few, though their leading principles and methods may be made intelligible to others besides experts. To many it seems a contradiction in terms to speak of popularising knowledge. A witty Frenchman classes together under one description those who would "make science popular, metaphysics intelligible, and vice respectable." Anyhow we may freely admit the dangers of what is called "popularisation." So far as it has led people to believe that they can take over the intellectual results of others, and appropriate them without an effort; so far as it has encouraged the acceptance of showy paradoxes instead of sober criticism, to that extent it is mischievous delusion. But this is in truth the vulgarising rather than the popularising of knowledge.

There is a genuine sense in which knowledge may be popularised; but it can only be done by one who has not merely accumulated but has assimilated knowledge; who is filled with its spirit, with whom it has become a living force, taking possession of the whole man, penetrating to the recesses of his personality, laying hold of him by his affections no less than by his intellect;

whose mental being is not divided into two halves, one of which resides in his books and a wholly different one in the outer world ; who keeps before his eyes the relation in which his own department stands to the whole fabric of scientific thought ; who can expound and utter what he knows in such vital form that it shall touch others with the inspiration of life. Books alone may give information, but not one in a thousand can in this sense popularise knowledge. You must fall back on the old Socratic principle, the method of human intercourse and the converse between minds. The teacher ought to be the subject vitalised and humanised in the presence of the student ; the science kindled into warmth and touching with its glow the expectant sympathies of the listeners. The electricity of thought ought to be abroad in the air of the class-room.

How widely different a thing this is from the false kind of popularised teaching which has brought it into disrepute among the learned ! We can easily account for the instinctive dread which the genuine Dryasdust feels on being told that he must bring the results of his learning before the popular mind. He cannot do so. His learning is a dead weight of facts. It is uninformed by reason, and uninspired by sympathy. "You must be above your knowledge," says Newman, "not under it, or it will oppress you; the more you have of it, the greater will be the load. The learning of a Salmasius or a Burman, unless you are its masters, will be your tyrant. 'Imperat aut servit'; if you wield it with a strong arm it is a great weapon; otherwise

'Vis consili expers mole ruit sua.'

You will be overwhelmed like Tarpeia, by the heavy wealth which you have exacted from tributary generations."

True learning being such as we have described, it is evident that many subjects which, if seized in their true relations, rank highest as instruments of culture, are least fitted to be brought to the sole test of examination. Such, for instance, is the department of classical literature. It is a subject that is many-sided, and whose value depends upon its scope and comprehensiveness, and on the wide horizons which open out of it. The classical languages, from one point of view, fall within the sphere of the exact sciences. The general laws of their growth and decay can be stated with scientific precision. On another side they are as free as thought itself, they look out over the whole field of human endeavour and imagination. We may come to them as grammarians, as historians, as archaeologists, as anthropologists; and to each class of inquirer they will yield results of the highest interest. But if we are to apprehend classical literature in its full spirit and power, we shall not approach it in the first instance in the attitude of specialists. We shall study it simply as containing imperishable thought in noble language. We shall not sever the language and the thought; they are not accidentally related. Most of the failures of classical education may be set down to the attempt to treat these two elements apart. To know the words without the sense, and to know the sense without the words—this sums up the character of the bad scholar and the shallow thinker. No: the language is the key, the one master-key, to unlock the thought.

But, you say, we may read the classics in translations, and thence get at the spirit and essence of antiquity, discarding what is outward and accidental. Well, one may no doubt learn much about antiquity by this means; and if one has a peculiar genius, one may even divine something of its inmost spirit, as has been done by a few men of rare imagination and insight, such as Schiller and Keats, whose knowledge has either been very imperfect or derived mainly from second-hand sources. But translations, the very best, are but shadows of the original. You cannot transfuse the life-blood of a poem into any translation. One language, moreover, differs from another—above all an ancient language differs from a modern—not only in outward form, but in inward and essential character. It is not that they express the same thing in different ways. They express a different thing, wholly or partially different, each in its own way.

Words are not coins which have an interchangeable value. A scientific term is capable of international exchange. The idea that it conveys can be passed from land to land, uncoloured by emotion, untouched by association. Each people can express it in exactly equivalent form. A cube root is the same thing to an Englishman as to a Russian. But the language of literature is totally distinct. The words stand rooted in the soil of national life, they are nourished from a people's history. Around them have gathered the accretions of thought of successive generations. The associations of poetry and eloquence cling about them. Words whose nearest equivalents are for us dead and prosaic stirred the pulses of a Greek and vibrated with memories of Troy and Salamis. How different, again, is the same word when it meets us in Homer and in the New Testament! To the student of language, one such word is in itself the epitome of a vast chapter in the history of thought, or represents, it may be, a revolution in our ideas of morals and religion. The abstract words which express intellectual moods and processes, moral sentiments, religious aspirations, are essentially untranslatable. They have no exact, often no approximate, equivalents in other languages. Classical literature may, therefore, be taught either from the narrow point of view of a grammarian who sees nothing beyond; or, starting from the basis of language and grammar, we may penetrate into philosophy, art, and religion—into all that throws light on the genius and institutions of a people, and fixes its place in civilisation.

None who have not themselves used and tried the examination test are aware how ill adapted it is to gauge the value of classical education in these its larger aspects. Facts that in the process of being communicated by the teacher had become vital knowledge; which had taken the colour of the pupil's mind as he advanced by tentative steps and slow stages and by frequent repetition of the idea, reappear on paper as so many ready-made results. They are artificially produced from a note-book by an effort of memory, and with the conscious intention of scoring marks. The candidate believes that these will be more paying than his own authentic ideas, which are probably immature and somewhat imperfect in expression. And he is unfortunately too often right; for examiners have to judge of answers by their actual worth and quality; and, unless they can detect a rote-like and unintelligent repetition of phrases, they cannot safely go behind the answers and speculate as to their source, taking off marks because they think that the ideas, or the form in which they are expressed, are too good to be the product of the candidate's own mind. We may here leave out of account the rare instances in which an original force of mind makes itself felt even under the artificial conditions of examination. But, speaking broadly, we may say that the formative process of thought is arrested as soon as a candidate sits down to an examination on literature, or even studies with a view to it. Second-hand generalisations and stereotyped judgments are put on paper. It is an inherent defect of examinations, that in certain branches of study they can do little more than lay bare results. They do not help us to trace the stages and steps of mental growth, to follow processes of thought, and to distinguish such as are vital from such as are mechanical.

A University, however, has other means besides examination of ensuring genuine work and of tracing progress along systematic lines of study. The Lecturer who is in daily contact with his classes, and who not only lectures but keeps to the good old custom of oral questioning, discerns the intellectual needs of his pupils, and knows of what stuff they are made better than he can ever learn from written examinations. The popular conception of a teacher's office is, some one has said, to help a candidate to play with a straight bat the most artful twisters of an examiner ; and there is no doubt that the dominance of the examination system has tended to create a wrong conception of the teacher even in Universities whose function is recognised to be other than that of an examining Board. An Oxford undergraduate, a Scholar of his College, was about to go in for his final examination. He went to his tutor to talk over with him a difficult metaphysical problem. The tutor discussed it on various sides, but produced no definite solution. The pupil at last told him plainly that this was not what he wanted. "What I want is the examination answer to the question; give it me in a precise form." "I really can't," was the reply; "it is a point on which nobody can speak dogmatically. Honestly, I don't know." "Come now, Mr. ——," said the other, "but you are *paid* to know." Yes, paid to know, and to put our knowledge in cheap and handy form for ready use and distribution,—that is the theory of those who regard University teaching as a commercial industry, and a University Degree as a "hall-mark" which ought to be easily purchased with the minimum expenditure of intellectual effort. To such persons knowledge is of value only if it leads directly to material advancement; and the different branches of University study, pursued without any sense of their vital interdependence, are only the means to a professional end.

But liberal studies followed in an illiberal spirit fall below the mechanical arts in dignity and worth. Arithmetic, says Plato, is an excellent preliminary to philosophic study "if pursued for the love of knowledge and not in the spirit of a shop-keeper."[1] The proviso here contained presents the Greek ideal of education. Intellectual training is an end in itself and not a mere preparation for a trade or a profession. The history of the word σχολή in its transition from "leisure" to "school," through the intermediate stage of "philosophical discussion," is the unconscious testimony of the Greek genius to the pure and disinterested love of learning. Greek "leisure" is sometimes spoken of slightingly as if it were the luxury of the rich or the dilettanti, an easy sauntering through life and avoidance of painful effort. But in truth it is not the opposite of activity, but a special form of activity, the strenuous exercise of the intellectual or artistic faculties. It is no state of blissful indolence, which is the ideal of some Orientals; no life of feasting, which is the ideal of the savage; no round of trivial amusement, which is the ideal of the man of fashion. It is work, genuine work; not, however, to satisfy bodily wants and the needs of animal existence, but to appease a pressing mental appetite—the desire for knowledge or the desire for beauty.

[1] Plat. *Rep.* vii. 525 D, ἐὰν τοῦ γνωρίζειν ἕνεκά τις αὐτὸ ἐπιτηδεύῃ, ἀλλὰ μὴ τοῦ καπηλεύειν.

Leisure and Work—the two ideas are to some minds inconsistent, but here is their point of meeting. "To do their duty is their only holiday,"[1] is a description we read of Athenian character in Thucydides. *To work their minds*, that too is their holiday, their true σχολή, the leisure that is worthy of one who is at heart more than a mere mechanic, whose energies are not all spent upon task-work done to order, with quick returns of profit as his reward, but who has free activities of mind which claim scope and play, energies which are voluntary, self-imposed, delightful; which result in the discipline, the quickening of every human faculty; useless, it may be, in the estimation of those who believe only in machinery, but for all who would not sacrifice the ends of life to the means, to be counted among the first conditions of existence.

A University is not an industrial association but in some sense a spiritual community. In the spiritual and intellectual life the distinctions of *mine* and *thine* disappear. We are rich not by what we have and keep, but by what we share. "Friends have all things in common" (κοινὰ τὰ

[1] Thucyd. i. 70. 9, μήτε ἑορτὴν ἄλλο τι ἡγεῖσθαι ἢ τὸ τὰ δέοντα πρᾶξαι.

τῶν φίλων) was the proverb which the Pythagoreans took for the motto of their school. They extended their idea of common property to embrace ownership in the spiritual and intellectual sphere no less than in the outward goods of life; and a far truer doctrine it is than the principle of unlimited competition in matters intellectual. There is no such thing as intellectual isolation. The worker in each domain should cultivate the power of viewing knowledge as a whole, and of discovering the bond of unity between the several parts. From one department of learning, light is flashed back in unexpected ways upon another, and studies which have long seemed unrelated recognise one another on a sudden as sister sciences.

New subjects will constantly gain entrance into an Academic scheme of study, and the labour of teachers and students will become more highly specialised. And it is well it should be so. That is for us, in our day, the road of progress. Only we must strive in the multiplicity of the sciences to apprehend the common principles of knowledge, and to keep the parts in just subordination to the conception of the whole; and this needs intelligent sympathy no less than grasp of intellect. The inspiring principle of University study is the sense that learning is not a dead tradition but living and growing truth. Never let us lose the idea of a *Universitas Litterarum*, of a community of letters—that indivisible kingdom of thought, whose several parts are not disconnected fragments, but are linked together in organic union, each essential to the joint action of the whole; which should be animated by one spirit, and understand one another's aims and methods. Only in this way can we hope with the growing subdivision of intellectual labour to combine the singleness of Truth, the real Unity of Learning.

THE DAWN OF ROMANTICISM IN GREEK POETRY

THE terms ancient and modern, classical and romantic, are generally used to distinguish two great periods, two phases of thought and sentiment in the history of European literature. True and expressive as the antithesis is if properly limited and interpreted, the distinction has nevertheless often been too sharply drawn, without due regard either to the literary affinities which are unexpectedly revealed between epochs of history separated by a wide interval of time, or to the fine gradations by which the transition from one age to another is frequently marked. Many critics appear to have assumed that in the classical world of Greece and Rome the individual was not yet aware of a divided self; the harmony of consciousness remained unbroken; there was a frank and unquestioning enjoyment of existence. The breach between nature and spirit is supposed to date only from the definite triumph of Christianity over Paganism. From that time forth there is conflict and disturbance in the soul, manifesting itself in vague longings, visions, doubts, disillusions; hearts and eyes are full of regret for something lost or unattainable. The tone of feeling grows more inward and intense, the accent more individual. Poets become self-scrutinising and self-pitying. The reign of reverie and melancholy begins. A perplexed twilight has succeeded to the glad surprise of morning.

The great change, however, which passed over imaginative literature under the influence of Christianity was not without preparation. Within the limits of Greek literature itself there are many premonitory symptoms of the new direction in which feeling was tending, of a new attitude towards the things of the heart, and another mode of contemplating the universe without. An exclusive attention to the earlier epochs of Greek literature has obscured the gradual stages of this process. The well-known essay of Schiller on "Simple and Sentimental Poetry" (*über naive und sentimentaliche Dichtung*) contributed in no slight measure towards establishing the contrast between the old world and the new under the form of too absolute an antagonism. He points especially to the altered feeling for external nature as one of the most significant points of difference between Greek and modern literature. It is "a strange fact," he says, "that so few traces are found among the Greeks of that *sentimental* interest that we moderns take in the scenes of nature and in natural characters. I admit that the Greeks are in a higher degree exact and faithful in their descriptions of nature. They reproduce their details with care, but we see that they take no more interest in them than in describing a vestment, a shield, a piece of furniture, armour, or any production of the mechanical arts. . . . They do not attach themselves to nature with that depth of feeling, with that gentle melancholy, that characterises the moderns. . . . Their impatient imagination only traverses nature to pass beyond it to the drama of human life. . . . It only takes pleasure in the spectacle of what is living and free."

The difference here is somewhat overstated. The generalisation, while true in the main of certain periods—and these the most distinctive periods of Greek literature—needs correction and modification if we extend the range of our survey. It ignores a process of real development that can be followed in the later course of the literature. Schiller knowing Homer better than he did any other Greek poet, and taking him as the purest type of Hellenism, has no difficulty in showing that the ancient or "simple" poet, living in unconscious harmony with the world outside, "*is* nature," while the modern or "sentimental" poet "*seeks* nature"—seeks to regain a "lost paradise" which has been forfeited through civilisation. The great period indeed of the Attic drama,[1] when the dialectic movement of thought was in full operation, can hardly be called "simple" in Schiller's sense; yet even then, as in Homer, nature is but the background of the picture, the scene on which man's activity is displayed. The change of sentiment, of which there are many premonitions in Euripides, becomes more marked from the time of Alexander onward. Nature is then sought for her own sake; artists and poets turn to her with disinterested love; her moods are lovingly noted, and she is brought into close

[1] *The Attitude of the Greek Tragedians toward Nature*, by H. Rushton Fairclough, Toronto, 1897, contains a well-classified collection of passages bearing on this subject, and many interesting observations.

companionship with man. The growth of the new feeling may be assigned to various causes; two or three of these, however, stand out with particular significance.

First, the old polytheistic beliefs of Greece had been slowly dying. The poetic instinct of the Hellenic race had from the outset given plastic form to natural objects; the visible world was broken up into separate divine personalities; round these beings grew myth and legend; as immortal men and women they had histories of their own modelled on the human type. The primitive myths, with a spontaneous sympathy which no later poetry has ever rivalled, express the sense of the resemblance between human emotions and natural processes: or rather, it is more than mere resemblance to which the myth-making faculty points; what is ultimately implied is the oneness of man with the larger life surrounding him. Not only wood and stream and hill are brought into human relations through the deity who dwells in each, but in the world of plants and animals also there is a manifestation of spirit life. Legends such as those of Adonis, Hylas, Narcissus, Procne, are the unconscious embodiment of impressions which, when translated into the reflective language of modern poetry, at once take the colour of romanticism. The Greeks were not, as is sometimes said, less sensitive than we are to the influences of external nature; but rather their sensibility, though keener, was less reflective. The feeling for nature is one thing; the utterance of it is another; and distinct again from either of these is the taste for landscape. No people has ever received such profound impressions from the beauty of the world around as the early Greeks. But the humanised forms into which outward phenomena were resolved intercepted their view of nature as a whole. The gods absorbed in themselves the landscape. The spirit of Greek mythology was in truth the precise opposite of the spirit of landscape-painting. As in poetry it tended not to the description of the outer world, but to the narrative of heroic thought and action, so in art it created not painting but sculpture. The river or the grove took the plastic form of the personal presence which dwelt in it.

In the representation of the higher Olympian gods the effort of the best Greek art was to efface, as far as might be, all traces of an elemental origin, to humanise the features, and bring them within the domain of ethical portraiture. But it was otherwise with those lesser deities who in the popular mind were still associated with the material world. The shape they assumed in art at once suggested their elemental substance. They became the embodied expression of nature itself. The river-god is known by the flowing outlines of his form. The breath of mountain and woodland follows in the train of Dionysus and his Satyrs, with their gnarled and knotted muscles and leafy locks. During the period comprised between 400 and 300 B.C., art, keeping pace with poetry, seeks to find fuller utterance for the impressions borne in on it from the world without. The vase-painter, while conscious of the limitations of his art in respect of pictorial capacity, does not rest satisfied with the abbreviated method of representation found on the earlier vases, where a fish signifies water, and a bird following the ship, air. He draws freely on popular mythology to express the anthropomorphic feeling for nature, the scene of the action being symbolised by the bodily form of the spirit who inhabits the spot. The sea is indicated by deities with scaly bodies and wavy hair, by Nereids holding a fish in their hands, by dolphins and other sea animals. The life and energy of the waves is depicted by winged seahorses and quick-moving Nereids. The splendour of the sunrise is portrayed in the personified Dawn rising from the waves with winged steeds, whose bridle-reins are of dark red, while on each side of the Dawn are stars.

A time came when the belief in the old mythology began to crumble away. The plastic forms of haunting and indwelling spirits, of Oreads, Satyrs, Tritons, Nereids, no longer stood between man and the world without. The traditional gods were hardening into symbols; they were becoming conventional types; and art and poetry, while they never ceased to employ them as the adjuncts of a story or as a decorative framework, sought their true inspiration elsewhere. As the mythological vesture fell off, the lineaments of nature herself were again manifest; the human form no longer projected itself across the whole field of vision. The eye could gaze once more directly on the visible universe; and though it never again could catch the same undisturbed and glad image that presented itself to an earlier world, yet there was in some sense a "Return to Nature"; there was the conscious desire to know her at first hand and to interpret her aright.

And now, in the period subsequent to Alexander the Great, with the increasing feeling for landscape arose an independent art of landscape-painting. Even in the fourth century, when stage-painting had made great progress, when the laws of perspective were studied, and colours graded according to light and shade, the conception of landscape-painting as a serious art was unfamiliar to the Greeks. This is shown by a curious passage in the *Critias* of Plato.[1] "For if we consider how the works of the painter represent bodies divine and heavenly, and the different degrees of gratification with which the eye of the spectator receives them, we shall see that we are satisfied with the artist who is able in any degree to imitate the earth and its mountains, and the rivers, and the woods, and the universe, and the things that are and move therein, and further, that knowing nothing precise about such matters, we do not examine or analyse the painting; all that is required is a sort of indistinct and deceptive mode of shadowing them forth (*σκιαγραφίᾳ δὲ ἀσαφεῖ καὶ ἀπατηλῷ χρώμεθα περὶ αὐτά*). But when a person endeavours to paint the human form we are quick at finding out defects, and our familiar knowledge makes us severe judges of any

[1] Plat. *Critias*, p. 107 B. Jowett's Trans.

one who does not render every point of similarity." The history of Greek vase-painting in the Attic period tells a similar tale. The separate elements which form a landscape — trees, rocks, water, buildings—are, if indicated otherwise than symbolically, indicated in a sketchy fashion, whether singly or in simple combinations. The several parts are present, but the idea of composing a picture is wanting. Not until we come to the vases of the Hellenistic period, especially those of Lower Italy, do we find a continuous background of landscape, and an effort to give breadth and freedom to the natural features of the scene, which are now at last combined into a pictorial unity.

The first cause, then, which prepared the way for a new view of nature was the dissolution of the ancient polytheistic creed. Foreign travel and scientific research contributed to the same result. By the conquests of Alexander a large intercourse had been opened up between east and west ; commerce carried forward the work begun by war, and the qualities and characteristic products of distant lands roused the curiosity of naturalists. Even China and India yielded their treasures to the scrutiny of the western world. Collections too were made of plants and animals, and the specialised study of Geography, Botany, and Zoology received a powerful impulse. The Greeks indeed had always united the love of science with the love of the marvellous, and their poetry in turn was quick to absorb the results of scientific discovery. The taste for geographical description, blending the latest learning with fantastic tales of wonder, meets us already in Aeschylus—in the *Prometheus Bound*, and if we may argue from certain fragments, also in the *Prometheus Unbound*—and even there it seems a little wearisome. A similar disposition betrays itself after the lapse of centuries in those laborious Alexandrian poems on astronomical and other kindred subjects, which appear to have had all the tediousness of a scientific manual without its accuracy. Still, the larger outlook upon nature, afforded by the discovery of a new world, combined with the patient study of natural objects, served a poetic purpose. The eye was trained by close observation to appreciate beauties which before had passed unnoticed ; a hidden feeling, which had long existed below the surface, was disengaged, and once conscious of itself, found imaginative expression in poetry and painting.

The influence of travel and research on the aesthetic sense admits of illustration from various epochs of modern history. But the nearest parallel to the movement of the Hellenistic period is that of the Renaissance in Italy. The Crusades had produced effects strikingly similar to those of Alexander's expedition to Asia. Remote countries were opened up. Collections were formed of birds and beasts and reptiles, and of every variety of botanical specimens. It was an age of naturalists. The earliest Zoological gardens were established at Palermo, and at the end of the fifteenth century it was not uncommon to find private menageries at the courts of princes.[1] In the sixteenth century Padua, Pisa, Bologna had each their own Botanical gardens. The scientific movement of the age carried with it artists and poets—Petrarch, for example, who was not only a poet but a skilled geographer, and is said to have drawn the first map of Italy. So closely interwoven were his poetic and scientific interests that from lonely intercourse with nature he derived the needed stimulus to intellectual labour. It is a noteworthy fact that the Italians of the Renaissance were the first people who felt again the charm of landscape as it had impressed itself on the sentiment of late antiquity, and that the conditions under

[1] Burckhardt, *Die Cultur der Renaissance*, ii. 10, 11.

which the feeling was revived reproduced in many respects those of the older world.

Of all the influences, however, which contributed to modify the classical Greek feeling for nature, none probably operated with such force as the rise of great cities in the Alexandrian age. The love of country life was one of the most original of Greek instincts. In the small city-state the citizen passed almost imperceptibly, and in the space of a few minutes, from town to country; his activities, public and private, kept him continually in the open air; and, even if as a politician he spent a great part of his life in the town, he had generally some rural interests or attachments. The long continuance of the Peloponnesian war broke in upon this quiet existence. The complaint of the countryman shut up within the city walls is heard in the *Acharnians* of Aristophanes. Dicaeopolis hates the town and is home-sick for his farm.[1] The commercial expansion too of states such as Athens and Corinth created a town life distinct from a country life. But the sense of distinction did not till the Hellenistic age widen into a full consciousness of opposition

[1] Arist. *Acharn.* 32:

στυγῶν μὲν ἄστυ τὸν δ ἐμὸν δῆμον·ποθῶν.

between the two modes of existence. Then at last man finds himself estranged and parted from nature, and a tone of sentimental regret mingles with the praise of rustic life.

Greek civilisation having been transplanted to the populous centres of the East—Alexandria, Antioch on the Orontes, Seleucia—the inhabitant of these overgrown cities hardly catches a glimpse of field and tree and sky, save in so far as gardens and promenades, laid out at enormous cost and with no slight artistic skill, restore to him some semblance of the works of nature. At home the Greek philosopher, Academic, Peripatetic, and Epicurean alike, has sought shelter from the outside world in the contemplative calm of gardens, which have become the property of the school. How far removed from the Greek of the Homeric age to whom nature was so close that he was hardly conscious of her presence; he did not seek her society, he did not avow his love. Political despair intensifies the pervading sense of weariness. The cosmopolitan Greek, detached from country and religion, is indeed free to gratify his own tastes, to develop his character, to be as individual as he pleases. But, though relieved from the demands, often so exacting, of the city-state, he cannot find a genuine satisfaction elsewhere. The feeling of loss comes over him. He longs for the ideal life of primitive simplicity, placing it sometimes in a legendary past, sometimes in a golden future, sometimes again among far-off and innocent barbarians, but always remote from the turmoil of the town. The fragments of the New Comedy contain many lines in praise of country life, its quiet and solitude,[1] and the tone of regret which may be detected there becomes more audible as we approach the Greek literature of the Roman empire. Dio Chrysostom (first century A.D.), oppressed by the sense of an outworn civilisation, throws into idyllic form the hopes and regrets which are of frequent occurrence in the later Greek rhetoricians, in his speech (*Or.* vii.) entitled Εὐβοϊκὸς ἢ Κυνηγός. He describes how happening once to be stranded on the coast of Euboea he was entertained at a hunter's cottage, where he discovered the repose and perfect simplicity for which poets and philosophers were sighing.

The meditative enjoyment of nature, fostered

[1] *E.g.* Menander, Ὑδρία, Fr. i. (Meineke iv. 207):

ὡς ἡδὺ τῷ μισοῦντι τοὺς φαύλους τρόπους
ἐρημία, καὶ τῷ μελετῶντι μηδὲ ἓν
πονηρὸν ἱκανὸν κτῆμ' ἀγρὸς τρέφων καλῶς.

by the new conditions of life in the Hellenistic period, affected forms of activity which might seem most remote from its influence. Hunting was a sport of the heroic age which had died out in most parts of Greece, but had always survived in Macedon. Alexander on his invasion of Asia found it already established there and pursued with the pomp peculiar to oriental monarchs. He and his generals joined in it eagerly. From Asia it was re-introduced into Greece proper, and soon it spread over the Hellenic world. It became the favourite relaxation of townsmen who, escaping from the city into the open air, roamed over free spaces of wood and mountain, and enjoyed the beauty of the scenery. Little was left of a sportsmanlike pleasure in the chase. Later, the Romans adopted it as a fashionable pastime, and cultivated it in the Alexandrian spirit, being themselves a nation whose instincts for sport (as Varro suggests) found fuller satisfaction in the circus. The extreme length to which this meditative temper of mind was sometimes carried may be inferred from a letter of Pliny's to Tacitus.[1] One day out hunting he fell into a mood of reflection—for though he killed three boars it was little more than an accident

[1] Pliny, *Ep.* i. 6.

—and by way of commentary on the fact observes that the motion of the body stirs the mind to activity; thus "the woods and the solitude, and even the silence which hunting demands, are mighty stimulants to thought."

In *Paradise Lost* Milton compares Satan as he enters Eden to one who has just escaped from the city into the country:

> As one who, long in populous city pent,
> Where houses thick and sewers annoy the air
> Forth issuing on a summer's morn, to breathe
> Among the pleasant villages and farms
> Adjoin'd, from each thing met conceives delight—
> The smell of grain, or tedded grass, or kine,
> Or dairy, each rural sight, each rural sound.

Some such impressions of delight must the pastoral poems of Theocritus, wafted as a fresh breath to the townsmen of Alexandria, have made upon them among their scorching sands. The idyllic scenes which he delineates are not mere pictures of everyday life, which charm us by the minute fidelity with which they render the happiness attainable within the sphere of a limited existence. True to the proper character of the idyll his poems pass beyond common reality. They re-establish a harmony between man and his environment.

The external features of the landscape are in inward correspondence with the action portrayed; and this harmonious relation of itself creates in the mind of the poetic characters, those passing emotions, sentiments, determinations of the will, which spring up in them without reflective effort. The dramatic situation and the dramatic movement flow, as in due course, from the influences of the place, whether the interlocutors be, as they commonly are in Greek idyllic poetry, simple beings who still live in unbroken union with nature, or more complex personalities, who in the revolt against the civilisation of the city have, at least for one happy moment, achieved the simplicity which is their ideal.

In either case the surrounding landscape is more than an artistic accessory: it is the soil in which the human sentiments are rooted; it nurtures and sustains the imaginative life of those who move upon the scene.[1] The Theocritean shepherds are aware that a perfect adaptation of outward surroundings is not only the condition of their placid well-being, but that on it too depends

[1] Euripides, as Fairclough observes, is in this respect the forerunner of Theocritus: cf. *Cycl.* 41 ff.; *Iph. Aul.* 574 ff.; Fr. (*Phaethon*) 773 (an early morning scene).

the inspiration of their song. They dispute in verse as to the spot best fitted for their rustic competition. Is it where the wild olive tree grows and chill waters fall, or where the oak trees and pines cast a deeper shade and there is the sweet hum of bees about the hives?[1] A similar idyllic rendering of nature is found in late Greek art. Even in vase-painting the progress of this sentiment may be traced from the fourth century B.C. onwards. It has reached a further development in the Pompeian wall-paintings, whose general characteristics, in all probability, reproduce the landscape-painting of the Alexandrian period.[2] The scenes by preference there depicted are not those which exhibit much outward movement, nor those again in which a dramatic conflict of motives points to an approaching catastrophe: rather, they are scenes suggestive of idyllic life—Paris on Ida feeding his flocks and declaring his love to Oenone; Apollo serving his time with Admetus; Polyphemus making love to Galatea. Sometimes the gods and heroes of mythology are represented as engaged in country sports or occupations — Aphrodite fishing, or

[1] Theocr. *Id.* v. 31-34, 45-59.

[2] See Helbig, *Campanische Wandmalerei.*

Ganymede and Endymion following the chase. The background is in keeping with the mood of the actors; it is designed to maintain that primary correspondence, without which the idyllic note of restful satisfaction would be wanting.

Thus the breach between man and nature has led to the desire for reunion; to nature man goes for refreshment and repose; and the conscious longing to put an end to the artificial estrangement finds utterance in prose and verse and in artistic representation.

Alexandrian and later Greek literature, touched though it is with modern sentiment, retains one marked feature of ancient Hellenism. The writer, whether of poetry or prose fiction, in his effort to draw closer to nature and imbibe her influences, does not, like the oriental or the modern poet, surrender himself unreservedly to the dominion of the outer world. He does not feel the pulsation of a larger life of which the human soul is but a fragment, or strive to catch in the grander or more solitary scenes of nature mysterious voices and intimations of something higher than man. The purely idyllic spirit extends to compositions other than the idyll. Nature and man hold converse, but only under favouring conditions, when nature is in one of her quiet moods. Nothing must be present to jar the senses or disturb the harmony.

The Greek of the Alexandrian age, like Rousseau, sought in nature an escape from the complicated rules of life and art, and a free satisfaction for the needs of the individual. He gladly welcomed the profound repose of nature in exchange for the discord, the turmoil, the pettiness of the world of humanity. But there the resemblance ceases. Nature did not for him, as for Rousseau, exercise her perfect spell in places where there is no conscious life, on the tops of mountains, in the depths of forests, in uninhabited islands, where man has never intruded. "Now," says Rousseau, "you know what I mean by beautiful country. No level land, no matter how beautiful, ever seemed such in my eyes. I need torrents, rocks, fir-trees, black forests, mountains, rugged paths up and down, precipices alongside of me which inspire fear."[1] Set against this the saying of Quintilian—as Greek as it is Roman in its spirit—that "natural beauty is found on the sea-shore, in level country,

[1] Rousseau, *Confessions* iv.

and in a smiling landscape,"[1] and we have two typical utterances of the ancient and the modern world; or rather, it may be, of the Northern and Southern nations of Europe. Mountains and lonely woods and angry seas, in all periods of Greek literature, so far from calling out a sublime sense of mystery or awe, raise images of terror and repulsion, of power divorced from beauty, and alien to art. Homer, when for the moment he pauses to describe a place, chooses one in which the hand of man is visible; which he has reclaimed from the wild, made orderly, subdued to his own use.[2] Or if uncultivated, it is one which bears the traces of nature's instinctive art, an art which needs no human correction. Such is Calypso's isle, with its harmonious wealth of life and vegetation;[3] such are the Elysian fields,[4] such the harbour of Ithaca, with the grotto of the Nymphs.[5] Up to the last days of Greek antiquity man has not yet learnt so to lose himself in the

[1] Quintil. *Inst. Or.* iii. 7, 27, "speciem in maritimis, planis, amoenis."

[2] *E.g.* the gardens of Alcinous, *Odyss.* vii. 112-132. In the descriptions of nature by Greek sophists in the Christian era the garden, symmetrically laid out, is still the ideal type of beauty.

[3] *Odyss.* v. 55-75.

[4] *Odyss.* iv. 563-69.

[5] *Odyss.* xiii. 96-112.

boundless life of nature, as to find a contemplative pleasure in her wilder and more majestic scenes.

There are traces indeed, even in the classical age, of a peculiar impression of dreamy melancholy with which the Greeks were affected by the spectacle of the sea. In literature the sea generally stands as an image of the inhuman indifference of nature, a type of all that is hard and unfeeling, from the time when Patroclus exclaims to Achilles,[1] "Pitiless that thou art, the knight Peleus was not thy father, nor Thetis thy mother, but the grey sea bare thee, and the sheer cliffs, so untoward is thy spirit,"—down to the days of the Greek Anthology, whose pages are full of laments over the unknown graves of shipwrecked mariners. But a seafaring and poetic race could not remain altogether a stranger to other emotions; and plastic art, in one of those less direct utterances which distinguish it from literature, records an impression which hardly perhaps came to the surface of consciousness. In the Tritons and sea-gods of Scopas there is a far-off and wistful look which seems to signify at once desire and regret, and is characteristic of beings whose life is that of the shifting, baffling, intangible element of water.

[1] *Iliad* xvi. 34.

Alexandrian poetry, less expressive here than sculpture, tells us of the alluring charm of the calm sea, as you watch it from the land. Such is the mood described in Moschus;[1] so too the Daphnis of Theocritus[2] sings beneath the rocks, "looking out upon Sicilian waters." On the other hand, when Achilles, in the *Iliad*,[3] turns aside from his comrades and sits by the shore of the grey sea, "looking over the boundless deep," he is smarting with grief at the loss of Briseis, and stretches forth his hands in prayer to his mother, the sea-goddess. Odysseus again,[4] prisoned in the island of Calypso, sits gazing over the sea; for across it is his home, and thereby only can deliverance come. There is nothing in this at all resembling the pleasant reverie of the Theocritean shepherd, a reverie, however, which passes easily into the pensive sadness reflected in the appealing mouth and eyes of those deities of Scopas.

In the long interval which separates Homer from the Hellenistic poets, the visible universe exercised an ever-increasing pressure and influence on the human spirit. Already in Homer the analogies between the world of nature and of man

[1] Moschus, *Id.* v.
[2] Theoc. *Id.* viii. 56.
[3] *Iliad* i. 349.
[4] *Odyss.* v. 156.

have stamped themselves on poetic modes of thought and speech. But the poet, absorbed in a strong human interest, is pressing forward with his story; he seldom delays to describe surrounding objects,[1] except indeed by one of those illuminating epithets which are flashed on us with the vividness of a sensation. Yet the profound feeling for nature discloses itself almost unconsciously in the simile, which serves as the connecting link between the spheres of the outward and the inward. The materials are drawn from heaven and earth, from land and sea, from the habits and ways of the whole animal creation, down to the minutest creeping or winged thing; from the delicate life of plants and trees, which are the immediate emblems of gracious youth.[2] Every object, every process and appear-

[1] Homer maintains a similar reserve in his descriptions of human beauty. This characteristic is noticed by Dio Chrysostom, *Or.* xxi. (*περὶ* Κάλλους), pp. 508, 509 R. Nothing, he observes, is told us of Hector's beauty till after his death in the words—*οἳ καὶ θηήσαντο φυὴν καὶ εἶδος ἀγητὸν* | Ἕκτορος. He adds, *περὶ δὲ τοῦ* Ἀχιλλέως *εἴδους οὐδὲν λέγει καθ' ἕκαστον ἢ τῆς κόμης, ὅτι ξανθὸς ἦν, . . . καὶ περὶ τῶν ἄλλων μικρόν τι περὶ ἑκάστου καὶ ἀνδρῶν καὶ γυναικῶν τῶν καλλίστων.* Something of the same reticence is a mark of all Greek writers till the Byzantine age, when the custom came in of describing exhaustively and with pictorial detail the various parts of the body.

[2] There are few more beautiful lines in Greek poetry than those in which Nausicaa is compared to the young sapling of the palm-tree

ance of nature, which can throw light on human activity, is noted with a sympathetic touch. For, after all, the purpose of the simile is to explain man's doings, to give definiteness and precision to the story, to present the image in sharp outlines.

Homer's similes, while unique in range and variety, agree almost without exception in this respect, that the picture of outward nature, animate or inanimate, is introduced to illustrate the action only on its external side. A direct parallel is very rarely drawn between the world of nature and of spirit.[1] The inward and deeper emotions

seen by Odysseus at Delos, *Odyss.* vi. 162 ff. Two fragments also of Sappho may be quoted in this connexion—Fr. 93 (Bergk) describing, apparently, a girl tenderly nurtured and destined to be a bride, under the image of the apple out of reach on the topmost bough of the tree :

> *οἶον τὸ γλυκύμαλον ἐρεύθεται ἄκρῳ ἐπ' ὕσδῳ*
> *ἄκρον ἐπ' ἀκροτάτῳ · λελάθοντο δὲ μαλοδρόπηες,*
> *οὐ μὰν ἐκλελάθοντ', ἀλλ' οὐκ ἐδύναντ' ἐφίκεσθαι—*

and Fr. 94 where the unmarried maiden, it would seem, is like the hyacinth, reared not in the sheltered garden but on the mountain slopes, trodden under foot by the shepherds :

> *οἴαν τὰν ὑάκινθον ἐν οὔρεσι ποίμενες ἄνδρες*
> *πόσσι καταστείβοισι, χάμαι δέ τε πόρφυρον ἄνθος . . .*

[1] The exceptions are two. In *Iliad* ix. 4-8, the divided mind of the Achaean host is likened to two winds contending for mastery at sea. Again in *Odyssey* xix. 518 ff. Penelope compares the movement of her troubled soul to the turns and trills in the nightingale's lament.

are interpreted not by the facts of nature or by the life of animals, but by other and kindred human experiences. Thus the joy of the comrades of Odysseus on his return to the ships from the house of the enchantress Circe, is indicated by a double comparison.[1] They flock about him as calves of the homestead flock about their dams with ceaseless lowing when they have returned to the yard. That is the external point of resemblance: the sounds and movements which accompany feeling have their counterpart in the animal creation. The emotion itself in its central essence and quality is expressed in other terms: "To their spirit it was as though they had got to their dear country, and the very city of rugged Ithaca where they were born and reared."

In the Hellenistic poets who watch and analyse feeling the simile is put to other uses. The inner workings of the soul have now become an interesting psychological study, and are brought into direct comparison with physical phenomena. Apollonius Rhodius, after contrasting the silence of the night and the slumber which had fallen on men and animals, with the tumult in the mind of Medea,[2]

[1] *Odyssey* x. 410 ff.

[2] Apoll. Rhod. iii. 743 ff., cp. Virg. *Aen.* iv. 522 ff.

compares the passionate movements of her heart to the rapid and flickering gleam of sunlight cast on the walls from a vessel full of water.[1] Here we have a direct parallel between the world of nature and of spirit, a kind of parallel as familiar to the poets of the decadence as it is rare in Homer. Such analogies had indeed already found occasional expression in the lyrical verse of an early date. In a fragment of Ibycus—to take but a single instance—the picture of spring-time, of the apple-trees by the river streams and the tender vine leaves growing in shelter, is set off against the storm of passion, as of an elemental force, in the poet's breast.[2] Euripides too affords a few similar examples, but these are as yet

[1] Apoll. Rhod. iii. 755 ff., cp. Virg. *Aen.* viii. 20 ff.

[2] Ibycus, Fr. 1 (Bergk):

> Ἦρι μὲν αἵ τε Κυδώνιαι
> μηλίδες ἀρδόμεναι ῥοᾶν
> ἐκ ποταμῶν, ἵνα παρθένων
> κῆπος ἀκήρατος, αἵ τ' οἰανθίδες
> αὐξόμεναι σκιεροῖσιν ὑφ' ἕρνεσιν
> οἰναρέοις θαλέθοισιν· ἐμοὶ δ' ἔρος
> οὐδεμίαν κατάκοιτος ὥραν, ἅθ' ὑπὸ στεροπᾶς φλέγων
> Θρηΐκιος βορέας,
> ᾄσσων παρὰ Κύπριδος ἀζαλέαις μανίαισιν ἐρεμνὸς ἀθαμβὴς
> ἐγκρατέως παιδόθεν φυλάσσει
> ἡμετέρας φρένας—

where παιδόθεν seems to mean "from the days of boyhood."

isolated utterances: not till the Alexandrian era are the hidden correspondences between the human heart and the aspects of nature more fully discovered.

Some stages in this transition can be traced and certain phases of the sentiment distinguished. In Homer, as we have seen, and, more generally, in the earlier Greek poetry, the simile is the typical form under which the likeness is indicated between human action and outward things. Metaphors are seldom employed for this purpose, and, when they do occur, they are of the simplest kind. The followers of the two sons of Ajax are spoken of under the figure of a "cloud of footmen,"[1] and then, as if the image were still wanting in clearness, it is expanded in the next line into a simile. Grief, again, is a "black cloud" that encompasses a man;[2] comfort or joy is identified with light.[3] Whereas in the simile man and nature are brought into direct comparison, but still stand apart, neither being merged in the other, metaphor, by the bolder process of identification, fuses together the two terms of the comparison—the two answering worlds, the inner and the outer

[1] *Iliad* iv. 274. [2] *Iliad* xvii. 591; *Odyss.* xxiv. 315. [3] *Iliad* xx. 95.

T

—so that the human action or emotion is blended with the material phenomenon which it resembles. As Greek poetry becomes more reflective, more observant of the analogies which run through nature, the range of metaphor is enlarged; it shows new capacities for revealing the manifold similitudes between man and his surroundings. The lyric poets pass beyond the narrow limits within which Homer confines this function of metaphor, and freely transmute the thought into the image. The tragedians, while they do not hesitate to employ metaphorical expressions such as a "sea of troubles,"[1] yet restrict themselves to such metaphors as are expressive of the simpler modes of correspondence. Hellenistic poetry, in its search for what is recondite in language, strikes out novel combinations. The description of the maiden Nycheia in Theocritus "with spring in her eyes,"[2] is one of the first of many phrases with a romantic ring and charm, which are freely coined in the Greek Anthology.

In the instances just given terms properly applicable to nature are transferred to man. But

[1] Aesch. *Supp.* 470; *Pers.* 433; *Prom.* 746; Eur. *Hipp.* 822; *Supp.* 824; *H. F.* 1088.

[2] Theocr. *Id.* xiii. 45, ἔαρ θ' ὁρόωσα Νύχεια.

there is also the converse process by which nature is described in language drawn from human life or from the larger life of the universe.[1] The most frequent example of such a metaphor is the transference of the word "sleep" to the repose of things inanimate. It is unknown in Homer; it occurs first in a fragment of Alcman: "Now sleep the mountain-peaks and clefts, headlands and ravines, and the tribes of all creeping things which the black earth nurtures, and the wild beasts bred upon the hills, and the race of bees, and the monsters in the depths of the dark sea, and the tribes of all birds that stretch the wing now sleep."[2] In modern poetry the feelings awakened by such a scene are placed before us in explicit

[1] *Il.* xiv. 17, (of the sea) ὀσσόμενον ("foreboding") λιγέων ἀνέμων λαιψηρὰ κέλευθα. Only once in Homer is inanimate nature clearly endowed with human emotion, *Il.* xiii. 29, γηθοσύνῃ δὲ θάλασσα διίστατο. In *Il.* xix. 362 γέλασσε δὲ πᾶσα περὶ χθὼν | χαλκοῦ ὑπὸ στεροπῆς, the word γέλασσε may mean merely "grew bright."

[2] Alcman, Fr. 60 (Bergk):

> Εὕδουσιν δ' ὀρέων κορυφαί τε καὶ φάραγγες,
> πρώονές τε καὶ χαράδραι,
> φῦλά τε ἕρπεθ' ὅσα τρέφει μέλαινα γαῖα,
> θῆρές τ' ὀρεσκῷοι καὶ γένος μελισσᾶν
> καὶ κνώδαλ' ἐν βένθεσι πορφυρέας ἁλός·
> εὕδουσιν δ' οἰωνῶν
> φῦλα τανυπτερύγων.

In line 3 the reading of Schneidewin is adopted for MSS. φῦλά τε ἑρπετά θ' ὅσα. Bergk reads φύλλα θ' ἑρπετά θ' ὅσσα.

language: the ancient poet merely strikes the keynote which asserts the harmony between creation in all its parts, and leaves the rest to the suggestion of the hearer. The same metaphor recurs in the well-known lines of the *Agamemnon*: "When on his noontide windless couch the waveless sea sank to sleep."[1] And again, but with deeper suggestion, in the famous fragment of Simonides, where Danae in the ark speaks to her infant child, whose profound slumber is not broken by the passing waves or the voices of the wind: "Sleep, I say, my babe, and sleep thou sea, and sleep my immeasurable woe."[2] Here a chord of feeling is touched which is rare in early Greek verse. It recalls to us the passionate wail of Simaetha in Theocritus: "Lo, silent is the deep and silent the winds, but never silent the torment in my breast."[3]

Conscious sympathy between man and nature is unknown in Homer. In this respect he is

[1] Aesch. *Agam.* 565:

ἢ θάλπος, εὖτε πόντος ἐν μεσημβριναῖς
κοίταις ἀκύμων νηνέμοις εὕδοι πεσών.

[2] Simonides, Fr. 37 (Bergk):

κέλομαι δ', εὗδε βρέφος, εὑδέτω δὲ πόντος,
εὑδέτω δ' ἄμετρον κακόν.

[3] Theocr. *Id.* ii. 38:

ἠνίδε σιγᾷ μὲν πόντος, σιγῶντι δ' ἆηται,
ἁ δ' ἐμὰ οὐ σιγᾷ στέρνων ἔντοσθεν ἀνία.

utterly unlike the poets of India, whose characters love to describe the landscape and mark the harmony between their own souls and the world around. Nature there becomes the witness and confidante of man's passions, the partner of his sorrows and joys. In Greek poetry, broadly speaking, we may say that the Pathetic Fallacy, as it is called by Mr. Ruskin, rarely meets us till the Alexandrian age. Some anticipations of the later sentiment occur in the dramatists, the most remarkable instance being in the chorus of the *Prometheus*,[1] where all nature, animate and inanimate, joins in a lamentation for the suffering god. We might fancy that we were listening to an old Indian hymn or a pantheistic lyric of the nineteenth century:

> All the land is moaning
> With a murmured plaint to-day;
> All the mortal nations
> Having habitations
> In the holy Asia
> Are a dirge entoning
> For thine honour and thy brother's,
> Once majestic beyond others,
> In the old belief,—
> Now are groaning in the groaning
> Of thy deep-voiced grief.

[1] Aesch. *Prom.* 406-435.

Mourn the maids inhabitant
Of the Colchian land
Who with white, calm bosoms stand
In the battle's roar :
Mourn the Scythian tribes that haunt
The verge of earth, Maeotis' shore.

Yea ! Arabia's battle crown,
And dwellers in the beetling town
Mount Caucasus sublimely nears,—
An iron squadron, thundering down
With the sharp-prowed spears.

. . . . .

And the tides of the ocean wail bursting their bars,—
Murmurs still the profound,
And black Hades roars up through the chasm of the ground,
And the fountains of pure-running rivers moan low
In a pathos of woe.[1]

Another and less obvious case is in the *Oedipus Tyrannus*,[2] where the scene of Laius' murder is impregnated with the speaker's own emotion, the place being regarded as at once an accomplice and a horror-stricken witness of the deed. The intimate sense of union between man and the world outside him, which is so often disguised under the veil of mythology, becomes more outspoken in Euripides. Numerous are his touches of modern and romantic sentiment. He feels an

[1] Mrs. E. B. Browning's Translation.

[2] Soph. *O. T.* 1398 ff. Observe the subjective colouring of *μέμνησθε* and *ὑμῖν*.

indwelling mystery in nature, and employs a notable variety of epithets[1] to suggest this intangible power that resides in earth and sky, in light and darkness, in mountains and streams, in fire and rain, in favoured places haunted by some divine presence. His descriptions frequently call up by immediate association the natural harmony or discord between man and his surroundings.[2] He catches the poetic symbolism of nature's moods. He notes the effects of atmosphere and shifting lights. He infuses a new wealth of colour into his landscapes, and their picturesque quality is heightened by colour contrasts.[3] His interest too in the animal and bird kingdom is tender and observant. The common bond of suffering draws them within the circle of human fellowship. "What bird," cries Antigone, "reft of her mother, perched in the topmost foliage of the oak or pine, will chime in with my grief?"[4] The halcyon[5] is

[1] ἱερός, ἁγνός, θεσπέσιος, σεμνός, δῖος, ζάθεος, ἀμβρόσιος, διογενής. See Fairclough, p. 52.

[2] E.g. *Iph. Aul.* 573 ff.; *Ion* 112 ff.; *Iph. Taur.* 134, 1097 ff.; *Phoen.* 1570 ff.

[3] E.g. *Heracl.* 854-5; *Hec.* 152-4; *Hel.* 179 ff.; *Iph. Taur.* 1245-6.

[4] *Phoen.* 1515-18.

[5] *Iph. Taur.* 1089 ff.

ἐγώ σοι παραβάλλομαι
θρήνους, ἄπτερος ὄρνις. 1094-5.

addressed as a companion in bereavement, and the tearful nightingale[1] is summoned to mingle her dirge with that of lonely womanhood. Helen in Egypt calls on the stream Eurotas to tell her whether the tale of her husband's death is true.[2] In the *Heraclidae* earth and sun and moon are bidden shout for joy over the coming victory.[3] Nor is nature unresponsive to her votaries. In the *Bacchae* the whole woodland thrills with a strange sympathy. The sombre and romantic setting of the play, its unearthly terror and beauty, form a background in keeping with the wild ecstasy of the worshippers; and when the Bacchants raise the mystic cry to their god—

> all the mountain felt
> And worshipped with them, and the wild things knelt,
> And ramped and gloried, and the wilderness
> Was filled with moving voices and dim stress.[4]

But the idea of nature as a sympathising spectator finds unreserved expression first in Greek

[1] *Hel.* 1107 ff. (ἔλθ' ὦ . . . θρήνοις ἐμοῖς ξυνεργός).

[2] *Hel.* 348 ff.

[3] *Heracl.* 748.

[4] *Bacch.* 726-7, trans. by Gilbert Murray, an expansion of the original—

> πᾶν δὲ συνεβάκχευσ' ὄρος
> καὶ θῆρες, οὐδὲν δ' ἦν ἀκίνητον δρόμῳ—

but true to the spirit of the context.

pastoral poetry. Theocritus tells of the herdsman Daphnis, "how the oaks sang his dirge—the oaks that grow by the banks of the river Himeras—while he was wasting like any snow under high Haemus."[1] Then comes Bion with his lament for Adonis: "*Woe, woe for Cypris*, the mountains all are saying, and the oak trees answer, *woe for Adonis.* And the rivers bewail the sorrows of Aphrodite, and the wells are weeping Adonis on the mountains."[2] Moschus in turn follows with his lament for Bion: "Wail, let me hear you wail, ye woodland glades, and thou Dorian water; and weep, ye rivers, for Bion the well-beloved! Now all ye green things mourn, and now ye groves lament him, ye flowers now in sad clusters breathe yourselves away."[3] The echo of these pastoral dirges is heard in Virgil's *Eclogues* and Milton's *Lycidas*, and in every later elegy in which nature has mourned her poet or her worshipper. Even Greek painting is not untouched by this peculiar vein of elegiac sentiment: by a bold symbolism it sometimes shadows forth nature's sympathetic emotion. In a picture representing the death of

[1] Theocr. *Id.* vii. 72 ff. (Trans. Lang); cp. the song of Daphnis, i. 71 ff.

[2] Bion i. 31 ff.

[3] Moschus iii. 1 ff.

Hippolytus described by the elder Philostratus,[1] the mountain peaks (Σκοπιαί), over which Hippolytus had so often hunted in company with Artemis, appear in human embodiment under the form of women rending their cheeks; and the meadows (Λειμῶνες) as young men, who let fall their faded flowers in token of grief. This abstract manner of personifying scenes and localities, without the aid of mythological legend or suggestion, might be further illustrated from post-Alexandrian art.

The passionate farewell of Ajax to his native Salamis,[2] of Antigone to the streams of Dircè and the grove of Thebes,[3] of Philoctetes to his rocky island-home,[4] might at first sight be thought already to betoken in Sophocles the modern sympathetic interest in nature. But the feeling of these passages, when read aright, is something different. For lack of human companionship Ajax appeals to the soil which nursed him; in the bitterness of his heart he calls even upon the hostile plains of Troy; it is the cry wrung from a lonely spirit. Antigone too speaks as one friendless and deserted: "Ah, fount of Dircè, and thou holy ground of Thebè whose chariots are many; ye, at least, will

[1] Philostr. *Imag.* ii. 4.
[2] Soph. *Aj.* 859 ff.
[3] *Ant.* 844 ff.
[4] *Phil.* 936 ff.

bear me witness in what sort, unwept of friends, and by what laws I pass to the rock-closed prison of my strange tomb."[1] Most decisive of all is the passage in the *Philoctetes*: "O ye creeks and headlands, O ye wild creatures of the hills with whom I dwell, O ye steep cliffs! to you—*for to whom else can I speak?*—to you, my wonted listeners, I bewail my treatment by the son of Achilles."[1] This personal converse with the world outside is for Philoctetes an enforced intercourse. A kindly sentiment has indeed sprung up in his mind towards the unhuman companions of his solitude; but the long years he has spent alone with nature have wrought no healing, they have not caused forgetfulness of the sweet society of man.

In the Indian epic, the hero Rama being exiled from court and cut off from the hope of his kingdom retires to a lonely mountain and dwells in the depth of a forest. His wife Sita and his brother accompany him. The vast and manifold life of the place finds gradual entrance into his soul, till on that delectable mountain, as he tells his wife, he no longer remembers his lost kingdom. But Sita is carried away and Rama plunged in despair. "The earth," he says, "seems to weep as

[1] Trans. Jebb.

if it shared in the grief of Sita. . . . The dark clouds and nights without moon or stars suit well the sorrows of love. The sun, veiled in mists, seems overpowered as I am with grief." Then as the seasons pass, the intimate communion he holds with nature, and the mingling of his soul with the universal soul, bring some solace and the calm of resignation. In the Greek drama we are still far from the love of nature for her own sake, or from the thought of her as an unconscious consoler.

The desire for solitude and wild places was for the Greeks of classical times a craving natural to a Satyr or Dryad or some other half-human thing; but in man it denotes mental malady—either religious frenzy, or a gloomy misanthropy which seeks solitude rather as an escape from fellow-men than out of love for nature. In Euripides, indeed, there is a feeling for the open spaces of sea and air and wild woodland scenery, which is almost romantic in character. But neither he nor any Greek of his age could have entered into the spirit of Byron's lines:

> There is a pleasure in the pathless woods,
> There is a rapture on the lonely shore,
> There is society where none intrudes
> By the deep Sea, and music in its roar.

Near the opening of the *Hippolytus* a dialogue occurs between the love-sick Phaedra and her nurse. Phaedra wishes[1] that she may be taken to the high mountains and the pine forests, that she may lift to her lips the stream of running water, that she may be couched beneath the poplars in the deep meadow grass. At the first utterance of the wish the nurse detects in it a touch of madness. This becomes more evident as Phaedra proceeds in her ravings. Soon the access passes off; she returns to her senses, and cries out: "O woe is me, what can I have done? Whither have I strayed from a sober mind? Madness came over me, I fell by some god's undoing."[2] The passion for solitude, associated with the imaginative love of nature, takes us back in thought to the far East on the one hand, and on the other carries us forward to the Middle Ages. In either case the sentiment rested on a religious basis—on the belief that the divine and the infinite could best be contemplated far from the stir of human life, on the lonely hills and in deep forests.

[1] Eur. *Hippol.* 209 ff.

[2] Eur. *Hippol.* 239:

δύστανος ἐγώ, τί ποτ' εἰργασάμαν;
ποῖ παρεπλάγχθην γνώμας ἀγαθᾶς;
ἐμάνην, ἔπεσον δαίμονος ἄτᾳ.

Alexandrian poetry introduces us to another phase of the sentiment. It is no longer the outcome of frenzy or morbid enthusiasm ; yet neither is it a feeling to which man in his normal mood is liable. It arises under the influence of love, which, if not a madness, is akin to madness. Love drives forth its unhappy victim into solitary places, where all around him he finds sympathetic listeners and spectators—trees, plants, birds, creeping things ; a miniature world which is the counterpart of his own soul, whose life in its most trivial accidents has a meaning and a message for him. Among the most interesting remains of Alexandrian literature is the love story of Cydippe and Acontius, which has been reconstructed[1] in detail from three sources—the fragments of the original poem (the *Aitia*) of Callimachus, the imitation by Ovid (*Ep.* [*Her.*] xx., xxi.), and the prose version by Aristaenetus (*Ep.* i. 10) in the sixth century A.D., which appears to be a singularly close paraphrase of the poem. Acontius one day saw Cydippe at a festival at Delos ; as in most Greek love stories, the first meeting is at a temple ; he falls in love at first sight—here again in accordance with the usage which after-

[1] Dilthey *de Callimachi Cydippa.* Leipzig, 1863.

wards became established in the Greek romance.[1] The parents of the girl do not favour the suit. Acontius flies from the society of friends and relatives and withdraws into solitude. He wanders through the woods, and sits beneath the trees. He cuts the name of the loved one on the bark. To the trees he cries: "O trees, I would that ye had intelligence and voice, just enough to say the words 'Fair Cydippe,' and that graven on each leaf ye had the letters which make up the name of 'Cydippe the fair.'" Each passing mood of his love is noted and analysed. In his lonely hours Acontius makes friendships with the trees and enters into communion with their secret life; he speculates whether he may ascribe to them feelings like his own. The language in which he addresses them is indeed a little unreal and far-fetched: "Dear trees, the homes of melodious birds, do ye too feel this love? When the cypress meets the pine tree does it grow enamoured?" and so on with other conceits.

[1] In Heliodorus, iv. 84, the fixed gaze which accompanies love at first sight is compared to an act of recognition: "For a long time they fixed their eyes intently on one another as if they were old acquaintances or had met before, and were attempting to recall the occasion" (*ὥσπερ εἴ που γνωρίζοντες ἢ ἰδόντες πρότερον, ταῖς μνημαῖς ἀναπεμπάζοντες*).

Strained though the sentiment is, and not uninfluenced by the courtly gallantry of the age, we should, however, remember that to trees and plants and flowers ancient legend had ascribed almost human susceptibilities to love, and that some of the most charming popular love tales in Greece are those in which the hero or heroine was at last transformed into some natural object. In any case the lover's flight from the world [1] and his colloquy with nature are in keeping with the prevailing tone of the period. So too is the specimen of the lover's dialect — that newly created vocabulary of fancy and hopeless passion which was bequeathed to Roman literature and then, at the Renaissance, to the modern world.

Alexandrian literature marks the transition from the poetry of action and of passion to that of sentiment. Literature in undergoing this change is but reflecting the change that had passed over the national life. The fervid youth of the Greek race was over, and with it the love of heroic deeds, the belief in great causes, the ardour of devotion with which the citizen sur-

[1] Cf. Phanocles *Fr.* i. 3, 4 (on the death of Orpheus):

> *πολλάκι δὲ σκιεροῖσιν ἐν ἄλσεσιν ἕζετ' ἀείδων*
> *ὃν πόθον, οὐδ' ἦν οἱ θυμὸς ἐν ἡσυχίῃ.*

rendered himself to the service of the community. It is the age of individual interests, individual culture, individual aims; philosophy is busy in working out the problem of the individual life; poetry takes the prevailing colour of the time. Its tone is that of reflection and heightened sensibility. It is on the look-out for emotional experiences; over these it lingers: it weighs and compares them. The sentiments themselves seldom have the energy or depth requisite to make them issue in action. They form a new kingdom of their own, alien to the instincts of the older Hellenes, one of hopes and regrets, of aspirations and delicate susceptibilities. Even where poetry takes the narrative form, as in the epic and often in the elegy, it passes rapidly from the action to the description of a pathetic situation. The outward deed is little more than a pretext for psychological analysis. What is presented to us is not so much the feeling itself, or the direct image of an object, as the reflection of the poet on what has been felt or seen. Of his own emotions he becomes the appreciative spectator. The emotions of others, even the most trivial, elicit a kind of sympathy: he enters into them more perhaps for the sake of tasting their quality than of participating in them. In a word sentiment is passing into sentimentalism. Theocritus is the last who retains the old Hellenic balance, the sanity of mind and body. His successors in the Alexandrian school soon fall away from the simplicity of the Greek genius, their delineation of feeling being often cold just because it is exaggerated.

A poetic sensibility such as we have described, always on the alert for the discovery of new sensations, becomes attentive to the moods of nature, quick to mark her passing appearances and to overhear in the world around the language of the heart. And now, love which in the more severe literature of earlier times had been held in abeyance appears as an idealised sentiment, and takes the first rank as a theme of song. It forms an integral part of the feeling for nature and blends with almost every landscape. The movement so begun perpetuated itself for centuries in the Greek romance, whose extant remains cover a period extending from the first century A.D. to late Byzantine times, the chief representative names being those of Heliodorus, Xenophon of Ephesus, Longus the reputed author of *Daphnis and Chloe*, and Achilles Tatius. These prose fictions have not merely a general literary kinship with the Alexandrian love elegies; they are lineally descended from them.[1] It was thence that they received their originating impulse, and a direct imitation of the Alexandrian models can sometimes be traced. The romances, indeed, brought a new and alien element into the poetic stories,—the element of fabulous travel and strange adventures by land and sea; incidents which were strung together loosely, and not woven into the tissue of the tale. The poems and the romances, however, agree in artistic structure and in the main features of the narrative. In each case love is the central motive, the soul of the story. There is the absence of a firm and sharp touch alike in the outward incidents and in the delineation of character. The real conditions of life are studiously ignored; the fundamental tone, the atmosphere of sentiment, is the same; the breath of a fantastic idealism floats over the whole.

As in other sentimental periods of literature, the hapless lover of the Alexandrian poets closely observes his own symptoms, and seeks a sympathising ear into which to pour his troubles. His

[1] See Rohde, *Der griechische Roman.*

passion feeds not so much on silence as on soliloquy; the luxury of woe, familiar enough even to the Homeric Greeks in moments of genuine sorrow, is indulged on slight occasion, and the words used cease to be any true index of the feeling. Antimachus the elegiac poet (*circ.* 405 B.C.), whose lyrical narratives had an appreciable influence on writers such as Callimachus and Philetas, sought comfort, we are told by Plutarch,[1] for the death of his beloved Lyde in verses which recounted the loves of others through a long series of disasters reaching back to the heroic age. In a similar temper of mind the Alexandrian lover narrates the sorrows of his own heart with as much enjoyment as if they were those of another. He is one of those who "live in wilful sadness." It is the kind of love melancholy with which we are familiar ever since the Renaissance, and of which Petrarch offers one of the earliest modern examples. Petrarch revels in his own sensibilities; he lingers over his passion with pain and delight. Like the Alexandrian he enters into close converse with nature; he desires solitude;

[1] Plutarch, *Cons. ad Apoll.* 9, παραμύθιον τῆς λύπης αὑτῷ ἐποίησε τὴν ἐλεγείαν τὴν καλουμένην Λύδην, ἐξαριθμησάμενος τὰς ἡρωϊκὰς συμφοράς, τοῖς ἀλλοτρίοις κακοῖς ἐλάττω τὴν ἑαυτοῦ ποιῶν λύπην.

he invokes the hills, the woods, the valleys, as witnesses of his grief; in the murmur of the trees, in the song of the nightingale, he hears the echo of his own heart; to nature he looks to be consoled and tranquillised.

The emotional overflow which is apparent in the fragmentary remains of the elegiac poetry of the Alexandrian period and the imitations of the Roman poets, is in marked contrast with the austere reserve of ancient Greece. According to old Greek feeling love was a disorder or malady of the soul, apt to become an overmastering emotion, robbing man of his power of free initiative. Lyrical poetry being in its essence the expression of individual passion, could not suppress the supreme passion of love, its ardour and its languor, its doubts, its hopes, its longings, its outward and physical symptoms. But love was not held fitted to be the theme of heroic song, either as the main motive of the epic, or the central interest of the drama. It forms indeed the background of the *Iliad*, but the *Iliad* is not a love tale; it is the story of Achilles, of his wrath and reconciliation. Achilles is no Teutonic Siegfried whom a romantic love impels to do noble deeds. His is the spontaneous heroism of the Hellenic people in their chivalrous youth; he is animated by the instinctive desire for glory, intensified by the knowledge of an early doom impending. Similarly, the drama, in its proper Greek conception, could not rest on so egoistic a basis as the passion of love. The struggle it depicts involves, no doubt, the destiny of an individual; round the individual the interest centres; nor, as so often in the epic, does the tide of events sweep into its current the fortunes of a nation. Yet the forces brought into play, those out of which the dramatic collision arises, are not individual caprices, they are no self-absorbed or personal sentiments, but the enduring interests of state and family, of country and religion.

The keen civic life of Greece, however, showed signs of premature decay; its turbulent liberty spent itself in faction; and when once the public interest ceased to be the first and chief concern of the citizen, no great impersonal motives remained to serve as an inspiration for poetry. The first tokens of the change are manifest in Euripides. The centre of the tragic interest is already shifting, and the drama is becoming the history of the human heart, as of a world divided against itself: it records the internal struggles, the claims, the imperious demands of the individual. When Euripides brought upon the stage womanly passion, with its conflicts and self-questionings—a love that was at once a blind impulse and a mood of searching introspection—his tragedy was criticised, and in a measure justly, as being a pathological study rather than a dramatic representation of life. He was in fact the first of the sentimental poets and the forerunner of modern romanticism. Love, that had hitherto been little more than an episode or by-play in a piece, now tends to be the soul of the tragedy. It is a new and independent power, asserting as it were personal rights, and claiming to compete with the established forces of the moral world, with the voice of law, with positive duties. Later tragedy, so far as we can judge of it, followed on the lines laid down in Euripides; it dealt largely with what Plutarch calls "the dark and insoluble riddle of love,"[1] selecting in particular such legends as easily lent themselves to a sentimental treatment.

If we looked only to extant literature, we should be tempted to imagine that romantic love stories were an entirely new growth at a particular

[1] Plut. περὶ Ἔρωτος in Stob. *Flor.* lxiv. 32, *αἴνιγμα δυσεύρετον καὶ δύσλυτον.*

epoch in Greece. But it is evident that rich stores of such material had been from an early date treasured in the popular imagination; and already in the sixth century B.C. Stesichorus had embodied some of these tales in poetic form,[1] thus anticipating by several centuries the love elegy of the Alexandrian poets. We read also of love stories associated with local legends at Miletus, Ephesus, Nicaea in Bithynia, Rhodes, and in other parts of the Greek world; many of these we now possess in outline, thanks to the industry of late Greek collectors. It is a matter of some surprise that the Greeks were so slow to perceive the literary value of this neglected material, becoming aware of it first, apparently, through the comparison of similar oriental tales, which had been previously collected, some as early as 400 B.C. by Ctesias. These native tales attracted the interest of antiquarians and poets in the Alexandrian age, and for centuries afterwards were largely drawn upon by writers of prose and verse. Pausanias who in the second century A.D. picked up in his travels many love stories from the lips of the people, concludes one of them with an observation which shows that the archaeologist

[1] Athenaeus xiii. 601; xiv. 619.

was fully alive to the force of the new motive which had subdued to itself almost the whole domain of imaginative literature. "Man is the only being for whom the prosperous issue of his love weighs in the scale against life itself."[1] Among the most beautiful of these popular tales are those of Paris and Oenône, of Hero and Leander, both of which were derived from current tradition or local legend, and almost certainly took artistic shape for the first time under the hands of Alexandrian poets. In their extant literary form, however, both belong to a later age, the first being the work of Quintus Smyrnaeus (probably in the fifth century A.D.), the second of Musaeus (probably at the end of the same century). In the case of the Paris and Oenone legend, we are able, as it happens, to compare the poem with the popular version on which it was based, and to see how the romantic interest now awakening added an accent of deeper tenderness and pathos to the original tale.

Even into the old mythology of gods and heroes the same spirit was infused. Poets who brought Olympus into the familiar circle of bucolic poetry, who represented Hermes as blackening

[1] Pausan. vii. 19. 5, *μόνῳ γε δὴ ἀνθρώπῳ ψυχῆς ἐστὶν ἀντάξιον κατορθῶσαι ἐρασθέντα.*

his face to frighten the naughty children of the gods,[1] who described Aphrodite hastily completing her toilette on the occasion of a visit from Hera,[2] and Artemis as a child of three years old sitting on the knees of the giant Brontes, and pulling handfuls of hair out of his breast[3]—such poets did not hesitate to transform many of the heroic myths into love tales. Achilles, who in the popular imagination had come to be the pattern of knightly love, is involved in a series of sentimental adventures out of keeping with his Homeric character. Here, indeed, it was possible to work on hints supplied in the older legends. The *Antiopis* of the Epic Cycle had recorded the rush of tender feeling which came over Achilles at the sight of his slain foe, Penthesilea. This was developed with romantic additions in later tragedy and in Alexandrian literature. Odysseus too, the love passages of whose career had been so lightly touched on by Homer, becomes a hero of romance: in one poem—the *Hermes* of Philetas—he forms a *liaison* with Polymele, the daughter of Aeolus, while staying at the palace of the king; an episode suggested, it would seem, by the story

[1] Callim. *Hymn to Artem.* 68 ff. [2] Apoll. Rhod. iii. 47 ff.
[3] Callim. *Hymn to Artem.* 72 ff.

of Nausicaa in the *Odyssey*, but conceived in a spirit the very opposite of the Homeric.

The ancient epic materials being thus handled in an idyllic manner, it was inevitable that they should be strongly tinctured with the prevailing sentimentalism. It was, however, a bolder experiment to introduce love into the epic itself as the main interest of the poem. This is the distinguishing feature of the *Argonautica* of Apollonius Rhodius. The love of Medea for Jason, as portrayed in the third book, is not a fantastic sentiment or the mere gallantry into which the Alexandrian delineation of love tends to degenerate. The account of the first meeting with Jason, of Medea's nascent passion, of the inward conflict carried on in the girl's mind between love and honour through a sleepless night, of her final resolve to quit her parents and her country,—this alone would prove that a new and mighty impulse had entered into poetry, and that an Alexandrian writer could touch at least one human chord in a manner in which it had never quite been touched before. It is not too much to say that the Dido of the *Aeneid* would probably never have been drawn as she is but for the Medea of Apollonius Rhodius — an imaginative creation sufficient to make amends for the weary spaces over which the reader is compelled to travel, for the outworn mythology, the tedious and absurd geography, and the dry and antiquarian learning with which the poet vainly endeavours to relieve the flagging interest of an action which is wanting in unity.

In another respect too, apart from the delineation of love, Apollonius Rhodius shows a modern spirit in his descriptive art. He is profoundly sensitive to the effects of air and light. The literature of the time was advancing on the road of realism; its heightened subjectivity made it more inclined to minute observation, and, instead of using the larger brush with which the classical writers give the impression of a scene, it attempted a rendering more detailed and exact. Above all poetry had come under the powerful influence of painting, and began to view nature through the eyes of art. Of all the poets of the time Apollonius is most observant of the diverse phenomena of light, of its pictorial effects, its broken and reflected images. In this particular he, among the ancients, approaches in a measure, and however remotely, to what Dante is among the moderns. In Homer the sun rises simply to "give light to gods and men." An epithet of the

Dawn, "saffron-clad" (κροκόπεπλος), or "rosy-fingered" (ῥοδοδάκτυλος), may suggest the illumination of the landscape, but that is all; the secondary effects of light are not described. Apollonius Rhodius seldom mentions the sunrise without some pictorial touch. For instance:—

ἦμος δ' οὐρανόθεν χαροπὴ ὑπολάμπεται Ἠὼς
ἐκ περάτης ἀνιοῦσα, διαγλώσσουσι δ' ἀταρποί,
καὶ πεδία δροσόεντα φαεινῇ λάμπεται αἴγλῃ—[1]

"When the gleaming Dawn shines faintly in heaven, rising from the far east, and the foot-tracks are streaked with light and the dewy lands shine with her bright ray"—

again:

αὐτὰρ ὅτ' αἰγλήεσσα φαεινοῖς ὄμμασιν Ἠὼς
Πηλίου αἰπεινὰς ἴδεν ἄκριας, ἐκ δ' ἀνέμοιο
εὔδιοι ἐκλύζοντο τινασσομένης ἁλὸς ἄκραι—[2]

"When radiant Dawn with her bright eyes looked on the steep heights of Pelion, and the crests of the salt sea waves were washed clear in the wind"—

or again:

ἦμος δ' ἠέλιος δροσερὰς ἐπέλαμψε κολώνας—[3]

"When the sun shone over the dewy slopes"—

or again:

ἤδη δὲ φόως νιφόεντος ὕπερθε
Καυκάσου ἠριγενὴς Ἠὼς βάλεν ἀντέλλουσα—[4]

---

[1] Apoll. Rhod. i. 1280 ff.
[2] *Ib.* i. 519 ff. [3] *Ib.* ii. 164. [4] *Ib.* iii. 1222-23.

"And now new-born Dawn at her rising cast her light high over snowy Caucasus"—

and lastly:

> Ἠὼς δ' ἀμβροσίοισιν ἀνερχομένη φαέεσι
> λῦε κελαινὴν νύκτα δι' ἠέρος· αἱ δ' ἐγέλασσαν
> ἠϊόνες νήσοιο καὶ ἑρσήεσσαι ἄπωθεν
> ἀτραπιτοὶ πεδίων· ἐν δὲ θρόος ἔσκεν ἀγυιαῖς—[1]

"And Dawn came up with her immortal lights, and dissolved the dark night in the sky, and the island shores smiled brightly, and the field-tracks afar glittering with dew, and there was a hum of voices in the streets."

Further he pictures for us the glimmering of stars;[2] the clouded moon as it appears in morning twilight;[3] the youthful form of Hylas as he was seen in the moonbeams by a fountain nymph;[4] the golden ray shot from the eyes of the children of Helios so that none can mistake their lineage;[5] the wavelets of dancing light cast on the walls from a vessel of water.[6] When Jason bears the Fleece through the night, his face is lit up with a ruddy glow reflected from its golden tufts.[7] In

[1] Apoll. Rhod. iv. 1170 ff.

[2] *Ib.* ii. 40 ff.; iii. 1376 ff.

[3] *Ib.* iv. 1479-80 ff.:

> ὥς τίς τε νέῳ ἐνὶ ἤματι μήνην
> ἢ ἴδεν ἢ ἐδόκησεν ἐπαχλύουσαν ἰδέσθαι.

Cp. *Aen.* vi. 453:

> qualem primo qui surgere mense
> aut uidet aut uidisse putat per nubila lunam.

[4] *Ib.* i. 1231 ff.

[5] *Ib.* iv. 727 ff.

[6] *Ib.* iii. 755 ff.

[7] *Ib.* iv. 172-73.

the same passage the joy of the hero as he handles the Fleece is compared to that of a maiden who from her upper chamber sees the full moon rising, and catches it in the folds of her fine-woven dress.[1] In another simile the magical effect is described of a radiant star, just seen above the horizon, on the fancy of a girl pining for her lover in a distant land.[2]

The art of this period runs a course parallel to that of its literature.[3] The feature of Apollonius Rhodius just noticed may be illustrated by the marked preference of the later vase-painters for representations of the stars, of Helios and other gods of the world of light, for images of objects as they appear through a shining or transparent medium, and in general for a new order of atmospheric effects. On one vase is depicted the rescue of Alcmena from a fiery death; the clear air is shot through with a rainbow gleam, denoting the rain shower sent from Zeus. On another vase, of Lower Italy, Helios is driving through a thunderstorm; the god stands on his chariot crowned with sunbeams, while on his left a thunderbolt is winging its way. Painting proper also occupied itself with

[1] Apoll. Rhod. iv. 167 ff. [2] *Ib.* i. 774 ff.

[3] See Helbig, *Campanische Wandmalerei*, p. 351 ff.

similar phenomena. In the pictures described by Philostratus the effects of light appear to have been artistically elaborated. In the representation of Comus[1] and of Cassandra[2] there is a play of torch-light over the scene; in the picture of Antigone[3] she is bending over the body of Polyneices, under a faint moon, repressing the cry that is on her lips. In another painting, the subject being Semele,[4] the figures of Bronte and Astrape appear, symbolising the fire cloud that broke over the house of Cadmus; the dark form of Semele is seen ascending to heaven; while the vision of the new-born Dionysus shines out against the murky flame. Not to multiply instances, the picture of the river Meles[5] had in it a wave arched by a light breeze into the fashion of a grotto, shimmering in varied lights beneath the rays of the sun.

It is, however, a notable peculiarity of Greek painting that while it learnt to delight in representing all manner of rare and luminous appearances, rainbows and strange cloud-forms and broken or deflected lights, it did not seek to render hazy and distant effects: the mountains that form the background do not melt into the atmosphere; the

[1] Philostr. *Imag.* i. 2. [2] *Ib.* ii. 10.
[3] *Ib.* ii. 29. [4] *Ib.* i. 13. [5] *Ib.* ii. 8.

outlines are not blurred; each object stands out in plastic isolation and distinctness. Helbig, who calls attention to the fact, observes the kindred phenomenon,—that the Greek language has hardly any words to denote the general tone and atmosphere of a landscape, rich and expressive as the vocabulary is in describing sounds and scents and play of light. It would seem, indeed as if Greek literature as well as Greek landscape-painting, in its mode of feeling and expressing the natural beauty of things, was conditioned by the clear sky and the full light of a southern land; just as, conversely, romanticism in its original and native force implies a northern air, in which outlines are less sharply chiselled, colours are more dim, where objects pass into one another by imperceptible gradations of light and shade—a world of half lights, of reverie, of mystery.

Not unconnected with this primary difference between the Greek and the romantic manner of seeing things may be the fact, that the Greeks of the classical age do not appear to have been imaginatively impressed with the distant prospect of objects viewed from a height: indeed it is worth observing that we have no record either in history or poetry prior to the Alexandrian period of any one except the Persian Darius climbing a mountain and surveying the landscape.[1] Aeschylus no doubt gives us in the *Prometheus* the sense of vast perspectives and wide horizons; and still more does Aristophanes in the *Birds* open up aerial spaces and convey the idea of far-off lands, of lakes and woods and mountains, from which the birds congregate.[2] But the first actual description of a distant view seen from a mountain is in Apollonius Rhodius. He tells[3] how the Argonauts made the ascent of Dindymon to do honour to the great Mother of the gods, and in a few brief touches he spreads before us the prospect that met the eye—the mouth of the Bosphorus, the hills of Mysia, the course of the Aisepus, the plain of Nepeia. There is but one phrase in this description which suggests the idea of atmosphere—the word ἠερόεν, denoting the haze of distance through which the Bosphorus is dimly discerned. It may be compared with the ἠεροειδέα πόντον, the misty or hazy deep, of Homer; it is again employed by Apollonius[4] to give the impression made by the long stretch of Libyan sand, that monotone of colour in which earth and air blend confusedly. One other bird's-eye view

[1] Herod. iv. 85.
[2] Aristoph. *Birds*, 228 ff.
[3] Apoll. Rhod. i. 1112 ff.
[4] *Ib.* iv. 1239, 1245-47.

there is in Apollonius, that of the world as seen from the celestial gates of Olympus—the life-giving earth, the cities of men, the sacred rivers, the mountain peaks, the encircling ocean.[1] Both passages imply something of a new pictorial sense of landscape in the larger outlook and the inclusion of a distant horizon. Otherwise they hardly depart from the characteristic manner of Greek description, its precision, its reserve, its brevity, the sculptural clearness of the image.

The vein of modern sentiment which lends a tender grace of its own to so many of the latest productions of Hellenism is nowhere more discernible than in the Greek Anthology.[2] In these, the fairest relics of expiring antiquity, there is a touch of intenser feeling in the appreciation of nature than can be discovered in any previous period of Greek literature. Strict limits indeed are imposed on the expression of this sentiment, partly by the artistic laws of the epigram itself, partly by the instinctive self-restraint practised by the writers, with whom the human interest was paramount over every other. Still we may recog-

[1] Apoll. Rhod. iii. 159 ff.

[2] In the quotations made in the text I have frequently adopted Mr. Mackail's rendering of the epigrams in his *Select Epigrams from the Greek Anthology*. (Longmans and Co. 1890.)

nise the various new sources, already indicated, of emotional interest which the outer world afforded. The citizen escapes from the town to keep festival in the country, where he lies on a couch of strewn willows and osiers, enjoying the breath of the west wind.[1] The quiet delight, too, with which Thyrsis in Theocritus looked out over the Sicilian waters is repeated in the Anthology. The Cyprian goddess loves to gaze on the gleaming deep from her shrine on land.[2] The dweller in the palace gardens on the Asiatic shore of the Propontis is filled with the "gladness of the bordering sea."[3] As in the idyllic poets, not the Muses only bewail the harp-player, but the river "Asopus stays his stream, hearing the cry from their wailing lips."[4] So too the pastoral dells lament the old bee-keeper on the hills, "the neighbour of the mountain peak," who was lost on a winter's night.[5]

Everywhere we apprehend the sense of natural beauty heightened by the alliance with art.

[1] Athen. xv. 673. [2] *Anth. Pal.* ix. 144.

[3] *Anth. Pal.* ix. 667:

καὶ πόντου πλήθῳ γείτονος εὐφροσύνῃ.

[4] *Ib.* vii. 412.

[5] *Ib.* vii. 717: αἱ δὲ τὸν ἄκρης

γείτονα ποιμένιαι πολλὰ ποθοῦσι νάπαι.

But the manner of presenting a scene retains on the whole its antique characteristics. An expressive epithet gives at one stroke some salient feature of the individual object, its shape or sound or colour, its appearance in movement or at rest; and such epithets bear the unmistakable mint-mark of classical Greece, differing only in the more decorative touch, or in the greater prodigality with which they are scattered. But the epigrams do not merely present a vivid image to the senses. The affinity of man with the visible creation is not obscurely felt, one of its manifestations being the enlarged sympathy which brings all living things within the range of the human affections. Still, so far as the inanimate universe is concerned, the perception of such correspondences in general eludes direct utterance. The old mythology is skilfully adapted to convey the impression; it is not yet emptied of poetic meaning. Pan and Hermes, Demeter and Dionysus, Nymphs and Naiads constitute the secret links between the outer and the inner world; in them is embodied the spirit of universal life, and in their movements we can discern the responsive attitude of nature towards man. In a few instances only, as in those already quoted, are external things brought into conscious partnership with human joys and sorrows, or the harmonies between nature and spirit suggested without the aid of mythical personification or other symbolism.

The love epigrams in the Anthology disclose another and more inward tone, as fascinating as it is surprising to the reader who has been accustomed to make a sharp distinction between classical and romantic literature. In Meleager, a native of Gadara in Palestine (early in the first century B.C.), whose temperament and genius are not without some Asiatic quality, love becomes a new and almost mystical ardour. In glow and intensity his verses sometimes approach to the early Aeolian poetry, though the antique simplicity is wanting. The colouring is richer, the imagery is often fantastic; the fragrance of oriental spices, the scents of lilies and roses are shed over the things of the heart. There is a subtlety that reminds one of the modern sonnet. All that is most inward and mobile in the passion or sentiment of love finds expression in him—the sweetness and the sting,[1] the honey that burns, hot tears to drink,[2] the gusts of jealousy,[3] the fire

[1] *Anth. Pal.* v. 163.
[2] *Ib.* xii. 132.
[3] *Ib.* v. 190.

and snow wherewith love pays for his nurture,[1] the wounds lately closed that are inflamed afresh.[2] Love is a bitter wave;[3] the fire that scorches the wings of the fluttering spirit;[4] he is the artist that moulds souls;[5] the master who tortures the Runaway soul;[6] and, again, he is himself the Runaway, for whom hue and cry is raised;[7] he is the Manslayer,[8] the conquering Deity that tramples on the neck of the fallen.[9] Love the Ball-player tosses human hearts for balls;[10] Love the Dice-player, a child in his mother's arms, plays away the lives of men.[11] Love is the unexplored sea to which all men are lured by the sparkling calm of Asclepias' eyes.[12] Love's draught is in the cup; the lover's wish is that the maiden at one breath may drink in his whole soul.[13]

The attractive and compelling power of beauty is set forth under many images in the Anthology. Myiscus is the sun before whom the stars quench

1 *Anth. Pal.* xii. 132. 2 *Ib.* xii. 80. 3 *Ib.* v. 190.
4 *Ib.* v. 57. 5 *Ib.* v. 155. 6 *Ib.* xii. 80.
7 *Ib.* v. 177. 8 *Ib.* v. 215. 9 *Ib.* xii. 48.
10 *Ib.* v. 214. 11 *Ib.* xii. 47.
12 *Ib.* v. 156:

'Α φιλέρως χαροποῖς 'Ασκληπιὰς οἷα Γαλήνης
ὄμμασι συμπείθει πάντας ἐρωτοπλοεῖν.

13 *Ib.* v. 171, cp. v. 261, the lines by Agathias, which are the original of Ben Jonson's "Drink to me only with thine eyes."

their light;[1] his frown is winter, the sunshine of his glance the first burst of spring.[2] Rash are the eyes that dare to drink in the strong wine of beauty untempered.[3] The grace of youth is as the unblown flower, still folded in the bud; it is the grape that has not yet grown purple.[4] Zenophile, "a spring flower among the flowers, the sweet rose of Persuasion, has burst into bloom."[5] As in the myth and poetry of early Greece, the feeling of sympathy with the animal world still exists: it is now more vivid and outspoken: there is a deepening sense that each living thing is a sharer in a common life. "To the toiling working ant" a memorial clod is raised near the threshing-floor.[6] The tame partridge that has helped the hunter as a decoy, is not left without an epitaph, when he has "gone on Acheron's last road."[7] A line of singular pathos tells of the voice of the singing bird for ever hushed: "Thy ways and sweet breath are prisoned in the silent

[1] *Anth. Pal.* xii. 59 (Meleager).
[2] *Ib.* xii. 159 (Meleager).
[3] *Ib.* v. 226. [4] *Ib.* v. 124.
[5] *Ib.* v. 144 (Meleager):

ἐν ἄνθεσιν ὥριμον ἄνθος,
Ζηνοφίλα Πειθοῦς ἡδὺ τέθηλε ῥόδον.

[6] *Ib.* vii. 209. [7] *Ib.* vii. 203.

paths of night."[1] But no member of the animal creation is addressed with more intimate affection than the cicala, the singer who "drunk with dew-drops" babbles in the solitude;[2] whose "evening hymn" (*πανέσπερον ὕμνον*) made the halls ever to ring with glad sound;[3] the musician who, when the string was snapped in the contest of the lyre, took up the lost chord "before the tune had halted";[4] the comforter whose wandering voice brings sleep to the lover;[5] the pet in the house, who at death has flown to the meadows of the world below and the "dewy flowers of golden Persephone."[6]

Family life, which in the Attic period had fallen into the background under the overshadowing interest of the city, is dwelt on with loving repetition by the poets of the Anthology. A romantic touch now glorifies the common things of the home. The prayer of the wife is summed up in two words, *ἀνδρὸς ὁμοφροσύνα*, "a mind at

[1] *Anth. Pal.* vii. 199:

σὰ δ' ἤθεα καὶ τὸ σὸν ἡδύ
πνεῦμα σιωπηραὶ νυκτὸς ἔχουσιν ὁδοί. Cp. vii. 212.

[2] *Ib.* vii. 196:

ἀχηεῖς τέττιξ δροσεραῖς σταγόνεσσι μεθυσθεὶς,
ἀγρονόμαν μέλπεις μοῦσαν ἐρημολάλον.

[3] *Ib.* vii. 194. [4] *Ib.* vi. 54.

[5] *Ib.* vii. 195. [6] *Ib.* vii. 189.

one with her husband,"[1] a far-off echo of the unapproachable language of the sixth *Odyssey*.[2] The retrospect of wedded happiness could not be more simply given than in the line

ἀεὶ δέ σφιν λώϊον εἰς ἔτος ἦν,[3]

"ever was it better for them year by year"; or the attainment of earthly felicity be told more touchingly than in the words of the dead husband who speaking from the tomb recalls his undivided home, the "wife that grew old with him," and the children

οἵ με κατασπείσαντες ἀπήμονα, τὸν γλυκὺν ὕπνον
κοιμᾶσθαι χώρην πέμψαν ἐπ' εὐσεβέων.[4]

Admirable again in depth of feeling and directness of expression is the epitaph on husband and wife, who died within an hour of one another, and whose common tomb is also their bridal chamber:

ἄμφω δ' ὡς συνέναιον ὑπὸ πλακὶ τυμβεύονται
ξυνὸν ἀγαλλόμενοι καὶ τάφον ὡς θάλαμον.[5]

No topic is more tenderly touched than sorrow

[1] *Anth. Pal.* vi. 209.
[2] *Odyss.* vi. 180 ff., the wish of Odysseus for Nausicaa.
[3] *Anth. Pal.* vi. 340.
[4] *Ib.* vii. 260.
[5] *Ib.* vii. 378.

for the young wife who passes from the bride-chamber to the grave:

> ὥριος εἶχέ σε παστάς, ἀώριος εἷλέ σε τύμβος,[1]

who in a moment becomes the bride of death, the same torches lighting her wedding and her funeral:

> αἱ δ' αὐταὶ καὶ φέγγος ἐδᾳδάχουν παρὰ παστῷ
> πεῦκαι καὶ φθιμένᾳ νέρθεν ἔφαινον ὁδόν.[2]

The gracious ways of children, and the pathos of their early death are a recurrent motive in the Anthology and in sepulchral inscriptions. On a tomb found near Naples, Hades is addressed in accents of bitter pleading, and asked, "Are not all mortal spirits thy due? Why dost thou gather the unripe grapes of youth?"[3] A little girl of seven pines away for her baby brother, who at twenty months old "tasted of loveless death":

> δειλαία ποθέουσα τὸν εἰκοσάμηνον ἀδελφὸν
> νήπιον ἀστόργου γευσάμενον θανάτου.[4]

The boy Callaeschrus goes hence to be "a plaything in the palace of Persephone":

> ἔσται μὰν ὅ γε παῖς ἐν δώμασι Περσεφονείοις
> παίγνιον.[5]

[1] *Anth. Pal.* vii. 600. [2] *Ib.* vii. 182.
[3] *C.I.G.* 5816. [4] *Anth. Pal.* vii. 662. [5] *Ib.* vii. 483.

A father and mother clasp the coffin of Cleudicus, a child not yet three years of age, who, "on an unknown Acheron" shall renew the youth he may never spend on earth:

> ἐπ' ἀγνώτῳ δ' Ἀχέροντι
> ἡβάσεις ἥβαν, Κλεύδικ', ἀνοστοτάταν.[1]

In the sepulchral epigrams of the Anthology, forming in themselves a rich literature, more perhaps than in any other part of the collection, a strange and romantic music lingers in the rhythm and phrases of the verse, even where the substance of the thought is not essentially modern. We catch this magical power of sound in such lines as those of Meleager:

> δάκρυα δυσδάκρυτα· πολυκλαύτῳ δ' ἐπὶ τύμβῳ
> σπένδω νᾶμα πόθων, μνᾶμα φιλοφροσύνας,[2]

or in the single line, with its untranslatable epithet:

> κεῖται ἀμετρήτων ξεῖνος ἐπ' αἰγιάλων,[3]

or in the epitaph of a sailor lost at sea, whose grave is known only to the sea-gulls:

> ὤλετο γὰρ σὺν νηΐ· τὰ δ' ὀστέα πού ποτ' ἐκείνου
> πύθεται, αἰθυίαις γνωστὰ μόναις ἐνέπειν,[4]

---

[1] *Anth. Pal.* vii. 482.
[2] *Ib.* vii. 476.
[3] *Ib.* vii. 376.
[4] *Ib.* vii. 285.

or lastly in the epigram on Echo, the mountain nymph, beloved of Pan, whose voice as it dies away is itself an emblem of the spirit of romanticism:

> ποιμενίαν ἄγλωσσος ἀν' ὀργάδα μέλπεται Ἀχὼ
> ἀντίθρουν πτανοῖς ὑστερόφωνον ὄπα.[1]

In a previous chapter we commented on the tone of melancholy that is heard in the Anthology. Even over the mind of youth there steals a romantic sadness. In Sophocles the young life "grows in those sheltered regions of its own, and the Sun-god's heat vexes it not, nor rain nor any wind; but it rejoices in its sweet untroubled being."[2] In the Anthology we find in the mouth of a boy the words:

> οὐκ εἴμ' οὐδ' ἐτέων δύο κεἴκοσι, καὶ κοπιῶ ζῶν,[3]

"not two and twenty am I, and I am weary of living": and the boy goes on to tell that he was in love. In another epigram a girl reflects on the happier lot of the young men who wander where they will, who can tell to their companions all that is in their hearts, and have games to beguile their

[1] *App. Plan.* 153.
[2] Soph. *Trach.* 144 ff. (Trans. R. C. Jebb.)
[3] *Anth. Pal.* xii. 46.

sorrows, while the maidens of the house are hidden indoors, "wasting away with dim thoughts."[1] The experience of age merely brings a more complete disenchantment, except indeed for the happy few who have found within the circle of the family affections the one pure spring of enjoyment left. After sixty years of wandering in many lands "from the sunset to the dawn," the last word in which the wisdom of the traveller utters itself is this: "I know both the grace of Fortune and the bitterness of life."[2] In reading the Anthology we become aware that the occasional voices which speak to us out of successive centuries grow sadder in tone; the eye is turned with a more regretful longing to the past; the future projects itself through a troubled medium of disillusion and of hope that knows itself to be hopeless. Life cannot again be a complete, a rounded whole, the βίος τέλειος of the Periclean age and of philosophic thought. It is a point in space between two eternities, between infinite time past and the time to come.[3] It is a perilous voyage in which chance holds the helm; the one certainty that awaits us

[1] *Anth. Pal.* v. 297, ζοφεραῖς φροντίσι τηκόμεναι.

[2] Kaibel, *Epig. Gr.* 640, καὶ καλὸν τὸ τύχης καὶ πικρὸν οἶδα βίου.

[3] *Anth. Pal.* vii. 472.

is the last anchorage below.[1] The firm reality of things seems to be slipping from men's grasp. Each day we have a different self; the self of to-day has no share in the things of yesterday.[2] All we know is that we were not and came to be: we are, and in death are not, nor shall we be again.[3] Nor is death itself the worse calamity, but to live ever with death before our eyes.[4] Life becomes a vision of men being borne out to burial.[5] The presentiment of evil, which casts a gloom even across the bright spaces of ancient Hellenic thought and art, is deepening into night. There remains by way of consolation, on the one hand the sombre philosophy of silence and patience,[6] on the other the imaginative satisfaction derived from contemplating dissolution, ruin, and decay.

Pater in speaking of the modern sentiment of ruins observes that it is already found in Joachim du Bellay in the sixteenth century.

[1] *Anth. Pal.* x. 65, *εἰς ἕνα τὸν κατὰ γῆς ὅρμον ἀπερχόμεθα.*

[2] *Ib.* x. 79.

[3] Kaibel, *Epig. Gr.* 1117 A:

> *οὐκ ἤμην, γενόμην· ἤμην οὐκ εἰμί· τοσαῦτα·*
> *εἰ δέ τις ἀλλ' ἐρέει, ψεύσεται· οὐκ ἔσομαι.*

[4] *Anth. Pal.* x. 59; xi. 282.

[5] *Ib.* ix. 412.

[6] *Ib.* xi. 300; x. 77.

"The duration of the hard sharp outlines of things is a grief to him, and passing his wearisome days among the ruins of ancient Rome, he is consoled by the thought that all must one day end, by the sentiment of the grandeur of nothingness, *la grandeur du rien.* With a strange touch of far-off mysticism, he thinks that *le grand tout* itself, into which all other things pass and lose themselves, ought itself sometimes to perish and pass away. Nothing less can relieve his weariness."[1] The feeling is in its essence as old as the book of Job. Job in a mood of quiet despair consoles himself for the perishableness of man by reflecting on the slow destruction wrought in nature—the mountain slipping away, the rock removed from its place, the waters wearing the stones.[2] The later philosophy of the ancient world taught the same lesson. Sulpicius in the well-known letter to Cicero on the loss of his daughter tells how he himself was comforted in a similar bereavement. He was on his voyage from Greece. "Behind me was Aegina, in front Megara; on the right the Piraeus, on the left Corinth: all of these towns that in former days were so magnificent are now

[1] Pater, *The Renaissance*, p. 160.

[2] Job xiv. 18-20.

lying prostrate and in ruins before one's eyes. 'Alas!' I began to reflect to myself, 'we poor feeble mortals, who can claim but a short life in comparison, complain as though a wrong was done us if one of us dies in the course of nature, or has fallen on the field of battle; and here in one spot are lying stretched before me the corpses of so many cities!'" . . . "Believe me," he adds, "I found myself in no small degree strengthened by these reflections."[1]

The same train of sentiment is repeatedly suggested in the Anthology. Antipater of Sidon, who wrote at an earlier date (*circ.* 100 B.C.) than that of the letter just quoted, sings of the past splendour of Corinth, its towers, its halls, its temples, all silent but for the wailing cry of the halcyons which fly over them.[2] Other poets in like manner celebrate Troy,[3] Mycenae,[4] Delos—once the centre of Hellenic worship, now unvisited by the passing ship,[5]—Amphipolis, the city much coveted of old on the waters of the Strymon,[6] Sparta where the birds now nest on the ground, and there are no sheep for the wolves to make their prey.[7] In one or two epigrams a wholly new

[1] Cic. *ad Fam.* iv. 5. (Trans. G. E. Jeans.)
[2] *Anth. Pal.* ix. 151.
[3] E.g. *ib.* ix. 152, 154, 155.
[4] E.g. *ib.* ix. 28, 101, 103.
[5] *Ib.* ix. 408.
[6] *Ib.* vii. 705.
[7] *Ib.* vii. 723.

note is struck. The spectacle of nature in her permanence and sublimity carries a deep solemnity into the heart of man.[1] The most impressive example is the epigram by the astronomer Claudius Ptolemaeus (second century A.D.) describing how he, a mortal man, the creature of a day, as he traces the orbits of the stars, is lifted above earth and admitted to fellowship with the divine :

οἶδ' ὅτι θνατὸς ἐγὼ καὶ ἐφάμερος· ἀλλ' ὅταν ἄστρων
μαστεύω πυκινὰς ἀμφιδρόμους ἕλικας,
οὐκέτ' ἐπιψαύω γαίης ποσίν, ἀλλὰ παρ' αὐτῷ
Ζανὶ θεοτρεφέος πίμπλαμαι ἀμβροσίης.[2]

Enough has been said to indicate some of the many anticipations in later Greek literature of a mode of feeling that is often regarded as distinctively modern—the taste for picturesque beauty in landscape and for subtle effects of air and light ; the attitude of mind that hears in the outer world the echo, the response, to human emotion ; a peculiar vein of love and melancholy, often fostered by solitude or by congenial influences from without, but growing into an independent kingdom of feeling, and absorbing in itself well-nigh every other sentiment ; a pity and sense of tenderness

[1] Cp. *supra*, p. 173.
[2] *Anth. Pal.* ix. 577.

towards the animal creation that reacts upon man, deepening his natural sympathies. These poetic utterances have not indeed the mystic depth of emotion, the strangeness, the intensity which belongs to modern romanticism. Nor in the poetic interpretation of nature have the more hidden analogies between the visible and invisible world been seized by the Greeks. There is no suggestion of a spiritual reality that lies behind the fabric of material things. The universe is not yet an emblem which the poet may decipher. It is not the garment in which the infinite Being clothes himself, the body which bears witness to a soul behind, the open scroll on which something of the divine thought is written. Still an entry has been made into a country previously undiscovered, which the modern mind has since explored and occupied. That poetry and life have been incalculably enriched by these later and profounder interpretations of the universe no one will be inclined to doubt. Yet there are probably many of us (need we be ashamed to confess it?) who turn back with fresh delight—not merely from Greek literature in its decline, but even from the great poets of nature in our own century—to Homer's simpler world, where nature and man stand out in clearer outlines, where there is no reverie, no vanishing perspectives, but "every peak appears, and the tall headlands and glades, and from heaven breaketh open the infinite air." [1]

[1] *Iliad* viii. 557-58.

THE END

PRINTED BY LOWE & BRYDONE, (PRINTERS) LTD., LONDON, N.W. 1